Cupcakes

NEW
HOLLAND

To Kayleigh
Happy Baking.
love.
CrM.

contents

introduction

Baking cupcakes and muffins is both a pleasurable and rewarding experience, not just for the home cook but also for the family and friends who gather to enjoy the fruits of the labour. So quick and delicious, they can be made when friends drop in or just on a whim on a lazy afternoon.

Cupcake or muffin?
What's the difference?

The Cupcake

Ease and simplicity have always been part of making cupcakes. Once upon a time, back in the early 1800s, they were called 'measure cakes' or 'number cakes' as well as cupcakes because the ingredients were measured by cup, not using a set of scales. It was a quicker way of preparing the recipe during a time when afternoon teas were a way of life. They also derive their name from the fact they were often cooked in a teacup. Teacups, often the second-best ones, would be greased, filled with a simple batter similar to a pound cake and baked in a wood- or coal-fired stove. Because the cupcakes were smaller than a normal cake, they required less fuel and less time to cook: perfect for a thrifty housewife!

The recipe for the cupcake has remained a fairly simple affair, although it's rare these days to see someone cooking them in old teacups, and they have evolved to become something slightly more elegant. From the simple beauty of a plain cupcake with plain white icing and a glacé cherry, to a beautifully decorated little cake with dark chocolate ganache and butter icing flowers, they're a way for the inventive cook to show off his or her talents and imagination. To many people, a batch of cupcakes is a blank canvas on which to paint and decorate, to show their true artistic talents – to others they remain simply a fast to make and cook and delicious cake.

The Muffin

Confusion reigns over what a muffin actually is. The word initially referred to a plain, flat yeast bun from the north of England. It was always split by hand, never cut with a knife, and was sometimes toasted over the glowing coals of an open fire, after which it was slathered with fresh butter. Yeast muffins are still made and sold in Britain and some of its former colonies, such as Australia.

Today, the word 'muffin' more generally refers to larger, taller cakes like very big cupcakes. These muffins originated in the US, where muffins were once also called 'gems' and were much smaller than the modern muffin.

They were popular across the US, and were filled with blueberries in the north-east US and huckleberries in the northwest. With the invention of baking powder, muffins got bigger. Today, the muffin is often still filled with fresh seasonal fruit, but adventurous chefs and cooks have taken the basic mixture and added many wonderful and tempting flavours and textures, from cherry and dark chocolate to marmalade and pecan treats.

The big difference between cupcakes and muffins is in the recipe for the batter. A cupcake recipe is generally plain and simple, and the embellishment and decoration go on the top. Muffins are not as showy, and are not generally decorated, but make their mark with the special flavours or fillings inside, whether sweet or savoury.

What binds cupcakes and muffins is that they are, and always have been, simple, easy-to-cook snacks that can feed and entertain a small informal group around the kitchen table, at a picnic or around the tea or coffee pot.

They really are a great way to explore your culinary creativity, as they're only limited by your imagination. Some clever cooks might consider decorating cupcakes with white icing topped with holly leaves made from green icing and red non pareils for shiny berries – a great festive treat for the holidays. For summer, a traditional muffin filling is blueberries. When the days are long and the berries at their best and in bountiful supply, they're folded through the mix and baked to reveal a golden muffin studded with sweet and juicy globes – a true seasonal treat.

Cupcakes and muffins are family-friendly baked goods – they produce consistent, crowd-pleasing results without blowing the budget or consuming too much precious time in preparation. Their simplicity also allows novices in the kitchen to learn the basics and gain confidence.

And they're great recipes for children to make alongside their parents or grandparents. Kids love being responsible for the bounty at the table! Keep in mind, of course, that children should be supervised at all times around knives, kitchen implements and hot stoves or ovens.

Cooled, freshly baked muffins can be placed in a sealed container, frozen and reheated later as work snacks or tempting weekend goodies. They can also be baked in several large batches to feed family gatherings (don't double the quantities: instead make several batches) or to take to community picnics. They really are versatile and fun!

Preparation

Before you start making cupcakes or muffins, or any recipe
for that matter, it's important to make sure you have all the
ingredients and equipment on hand.

First take a little time to read the recipe from beginning to end. Although a lot of the
recipes in this book use similar methods, there may be subtle differences. Next, check
through the ingredients and make sure you have enough of each. There's nothing
worse than starting a recipe only to find you have to go to the store for more sugar!

Allow ingredients stored in the refrigerator, such as butter and eggs, to come to
room temperature before using: cold ingredients can cause the mix to contract and
become tough.

Many people prefer the rich flavour and moist texture that full-fat milk gives to their
cooking, although the more health-conscious will prefer to use skimmed or low-
fat milk. Either way, once again the milk should be at room temperature. A handy
method is to measure out the required amount of milk, cover it with plastic wrap and
leave it out to come to room temperature, so they can return the carton or bottle to
the refrigerator to keep it fresh.

Cupcake papers are little paper cups with pleated edges, in which the cupcake or muffin batter can be poured and then put in the oven for baking. Quality cupcake papers are a boon. Look for ones with thick paper that will keep its shape during its time in the oven. Some of the quality papers have the name 'Muffin' or 'Cupcake' printed in attractive letters on the side. Thin papers don't hold their shape – for the novice baker, using them can result in a wasteful mess of baked mix and paper! To avoid this, papers are best dropped into a muffin tray, which will keep everything perfectly in place.

If you don't have a muffin tray, always place the papers on an ovenproof tray – this will keep them together and stop any spills from spoiling the bottom of the oven. Position the papers close together, so they can help each other hold their shape.

If you plan on doing a lot of baking, it's a good idea to spend a little extra money and get a good, durable muffin tray. Grease the trays well before you bake, and make sure they're not hot, as this can start the baking powder working too early!

With good, wholesome ingredients and these great recipes you'll have many happy hours of baking.

Almost time to turn on the oven!

The tradition of home baking has always been about putting good food on the table. When the cakes are brought out and the tea or coffee is served, it's an occasion for family, neighbours and friends to take time to sit down and talk, to be with each other and to listen, laugh, remember old times and plan new events.

The smell of freshly baked goods, and the aromas of spices wafting through the air, create an environment of gentle anticipation which will please and excite the young and the young at heart.

To create the perfect cupcake or muffin time after time, there are a few simple rules to follow.

Sift the dry ingredients together and make sure they are mixed through thoroughly. Lumps in the flour in the early stages can cause hard, white lumps to end up in the final mix, which is not a desirable outcome.

Baking powder, if poorly mixed through, can react with the skin of fruits and nuts such as raspberries, blueberries and walnuts, causing natural dyes to leach out of the ingredients – resulting in blue or green stains in the muffins. Although these stains are perfectly harmless, they indicate that perhaps a little more care and gentle handling is needed during the preparation stage!

Do not over-work the mix beyond the time recommended in the method of the recipe. This makes the proteins in the flour (ie gluten) stick together, meaning the mix will be too strong and tough and won't rise. The lightest touch possible should be used!

Nuts make nutritious, energy-packed highlights in a muffin and a delicious crowning glory for a cupcake. To get the best from nuts, ensure they're fresh and give them a gentle toasting in a warm oven for a few minutes to bring out their taste. Evenly spread the nuts over an ovenproof tray covered with oven paper. Toast almonds and hazelnuts at 350°F/180°C for 10 minutes. Walnuts and pecans should be toasted a little more gently, at 320°F/160°C for 10 minutes, and macadamias at 300°F/150°C for the same period. Keep an eye on the nuts as you toast them, too, as they can burn very rapidly if left unattended. They should develop a lovely golden hue, but nothing darker.

This technique for toasting nuts may be used for other dishes, where you need a little extra taste from them.

Remember to not overload the muffins with extra fillings – sometimes it can be too much of a good thing! Fold in added ingredients such as chocolate and nuts after the batter is made, to help distribute them evenly. If you add the fillings to the dry ingredients, the flour will stick to the nuts or bits of chocolate, stopping them from becoming part of the dough.

There's nothing worse than biting into a muffin to find that all the ingredients have unexpectedly sunk to the bottom of your muffin.

Some people use an ice-cream scoop to spoon the mixture into the cupcake papers. This is a good way of getting a decent-sized portion of mixture into the tray or paper in one go. Make sure you follow the directions and only use the amount of mix directed, as too much cupcake or muffin mix will cause the mix to rise up and over the sides of the paper or tray, creating mushroom-shaped cakes. Also make sure your cupcake papers are in place before you fill them, as they don't move easily with batter in them.

To make cleaning a lot easier, a little bit of cooking oil can be used to coat utensils before use. A cheese grater, if lightly brushed with a neutral cooking oil such as canola or sunflower seed oil, will clean up much more easily. If you plan on using honey, maple syrup, golden syrup or treacle, a little oil brushed on the cup or measuring spoon will stop the sticky liquid from adhering, making for a more accurate measure and less time at the sink.

When baking, note that not all ovens are the same and that cooking times can vary. In non-fan-forced ovens, the cupcakes on the inside of the tray take slightly longer to cook, so by the time they are ready the ones on the outside may be slightly deeper golden. A good rule of thumb is to insert a fine skewer into the cupcake – if it's ready, the skewer will come out clean. With experience you'll be able to judge with your eyes and nose when they are baked to perfection.

Muffins are always best served warm. Some people like to put on a little bit of extra fresh butter and let it melt into the warm dough.

Keep leftover muffins covered with a clean dishcloth. This will keep them fresh and stop them from going sticky. They can be refrigerated like this for a few days and warmed a little in a microwave before serving. Don't store them in a sealed container unless you're freezing them.

Once they're cooled, you can freeze muffins in a tightly sealed container: they'll keep well for about a month. To serve, defrost and place on a tray in a warm oven at 300°F/150°C for 15 minutes.

With decorating, there's no right or wrong. You'll need a spatula and plenty of fresh warm water to sculpt and spread the icing across the top of the cupcake. For applying icing in patterns, you can start off using a sturdy plastic bag with a tiny hole snipped off one corner – it's rough and ready but OK to get you started. You'll have more control with a good icing bag or gun and a set of nozzles, though. Some nozzles are cut and moulded to allow the production of flowers and leaves and other shapes. Value-for-money icing kits can be purchased from good food stores and department stores.

Make sure your nozzles are cleaned properly with plenty of warm water straight after use, as set icing is harder to clean away than fresh.

Cupcakes are at their best fresh after cooling on a wire rack. When decorating, handle the cupcakes by their base, as this is their strongest point.

Chocolate is a joy to eat and a popular decoration. Melted dark chocolate can be used to drizzle delectable patterns over contrasting white icing.

Chocolate can be melted in a ceramic cup in the microwave, but the traditional method is still the best. Break the chocolate up into small pieces and put it in a heatproof bowl sitting on top of a saucepan containing barely simmering hot water (a double-boiler). Stir the chocolate as it melts and never ever let water get into chocolate, as this will cause it to become granular.

If you do end up with water in your chocolate, add a dash of cooking oil to help the chocolate return to the desired texture.

In the following pages we've included a basic explanation of how to prepare a piping bag. It's a handy skill if you have a piece of baking paper around, but if you find it a bit fiddly or you don't have any paper on hand, the back-up trick is to fill the corner of a small plastic bag, simply roll it up and snip off the point. As long as the bag is sturdy enough and the person controlling the piping is gentle enough, the humble plastic bag can work wonderfully for applying line decorations or writing messages on individual cakes.

Preparing a plastic bag for piping

1 Take a sturdy, small-to medium-sized plastic bag, place the icing or warm chocolate into one corner and gently remove any air from the bag.

2 Fold over then roll down the top of the plastic bag on a diagonal angle, toward the filled corner that you will write from.

3 Snip a small piece of plastic from the corner of the bag to allow the icing to flow. Control the icing by applying more or less pressure to the rolled-up back part of the bag.

Making a paper piping bag

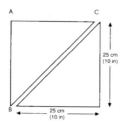

1 Cut a 25cm square of greaseproof paper. Cut the square in half diagonally to form two triangles. To make the piping bag, place the paper triangles on top of each other and mark the three corners A, B and C.

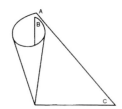

2 Fold corner B around and inside corner A.

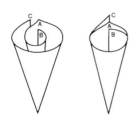

3 Bring corner C around the outside of the bag until it fits exactly behind corner A. At this stage all three corners should be together and the point closed.

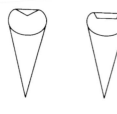

4 Fold corner A over two or three times to hold the bag together. Snip the point off the bag and drop into an icing nozzle. The piping bag can also be used without a nozzle for writing and outlines, in which case only the very tip of the point should be snipped off.

Once you've made a few of these recipes you'll find the ones you love and come back to them time and time again. They'll become your family staples! You might even want to experiment by changing the decorations, the flavourings or toppings. You'll have cakes that you've made with skill in your own kitchen that will please friends and family, and when you have your favourite recipes they can be made for unexpected guests at the drop of the hat.

stay organised
but have fun...

- Make sure all the ingredients are by your side, the equipment is ready and the oven is preheating before you start cooking.
- Let your imagination run free and use these recipes to make the cupcakes and muffins as a starting point.
- Relax and remember: the age-old art of home baking is about pleasure and giving.

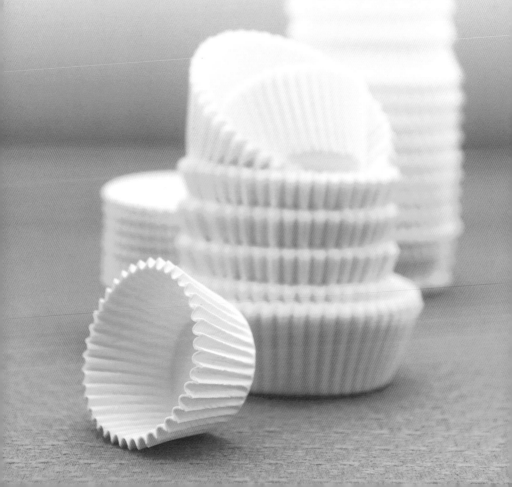

vanilla cupcakes

If the cupcake is used as a traditional tea cake, then nothing works better than vanilla at a tea party. Vanilla cakes married with whipped butter cream icing and white chocolate pieces is the perfect accompaniment to an afternoon gathering. This chapter will show you some of the more basic cupcakes and traditional toppings to get you started along the journey of quality home baking.

Double White Cupcakes

Vanilla Butter Cupcakes

White Chocolate and Buttermilk Cupcakes

Persian Vanilla Cupcakes

Marshmallow Vanilla Buttercups

Buttermilk Bootie Cupcakes

Vanilla Rose Cupcakes

Lavender Buttercream Cupcakes

Vanilla Heart Cupcakes

White Musk Cupcakes

Triple White Cupcakes

Double white cupcakes

3 eggs
½ cup butter, softened
1 cup superfine/caster sugar
½ cup milk
1½ cups bakers/self-raising flour,
    sifted
3½ oz/100g white chocolate,
    grated
1 teaspoon vanilla extract

TOPPING
1½ cups confectioners'/icing
    sugar
½ cup butter, softened
72 pre-made meringue
    decorations (with silver balls)

1. Preheat the oven to 320°F/160°C.
   Line a 12-cupcake pan with cupcake
   papers. In a medium-sized bowl, lightly
   beat the eggs, add butter and sugar,
   then mix until light and fluffy.
2. Add the milk, flour, chocolate and
   vanilla, and stir to combine. Beat with
   an electric mixer for 2 minutes, until
   light and creamy.
3. Divide the mixture evenly between the
   cake papers. Bake for 18–20 minutes
   until risen and firm to touch. Allow to
   cool for a few minutes and then transfer
   to a wire rack. Allow to cool fully before
   icing.

TOPPING
1. Meanwhile, combine the sugar and
   butter; beat with a wooden spoon until
   light and fluffy. Spoon onto cupcakes,
   add decorations.

Vanilla butter cupcakes

MAKES 12

1. Preheat the oven to 320°F/160°C. Line a 12-cupcake pan with cupcake papers. In a medium-sized bowl, lightly beat the eggs, add butter and sugar, then mix until light and fluffy.
2. Add buttermilk, flour and vanilla, and stir to combine. Beat with an electric mixer for 2 minutes, until light and creamy.
3. Divide the mixture evenly between the cake papers. Bake for 18–20 minutes until risen and firm to touch. Allow to cool for a few minutes and then transfer to a wire rack. Allow to cool fully before icing.

TOPPING

1. Meanwhile, combine half the topping ingredients except sprinkles and stir with a wooden spoon until mixed together. Add remaining ingredients and beat with the spoon until light and fluffy.
2. Spoon topping onto cakes using the back of a spoon. Decorate with coloured sprinkles.

3 eggs
½ cup butter, softened
1 cup superfine/caster sugar
½ cup buttermilk
1½ cups bakers/self-raising flour, sifted
1 teaspoon vanilla extract

TOPPING
1½ cups confectioners'/icing sugar
½ cup butter, softened
6 drops vanilla extract
coloured confectionery sprinkles (available from cake decoration stores)

White chocolate and buttermilk cupcakes

MAKES 12

3 eggs
½ cup butter, softened
1 cup superfine/caster sugar
½ cup buttermilk
1½ cups bakers/self-raising flour, sifted
1 teaspoon vanilla extract

TOPPING
3½ oz/100g white chocolate, coarsely grated
1 tablespoon butter, softened
⅓ cup cream, thickened
candied frangipanis (available from cake decoration stores)

1. Preheat the oven to 320°F/160°C. Line a 12-cupcake pan with cupcake papers. In a medium-sized bowl, lightly beat the eggs, add butter and sugar, then mix until light and fluffy.
2. Add buttermilk, flour and vanilla, and stir to combine. Beat with an electric mixer for 2 minutes, until light and creamy.
3. Divide the mixture evenly between the cake papers. Bake for 18–20 minutes until risen and firm to touch. Allow to cool for a few minutes and then transfer to a wire rack. Allow to cool fully before icing.

TOPPING
1. Meanwhile, combine the chocolate and butter in a medium-sized saucepan over a medium heat. As the mixture begins to melt, add the cream slowly, then reduce heat to low, stirring constantly, until mixture thickens.
2. Remove from heat and cool. Spread evenly onto cupcakes with a teaspoon and then top with frangipani decorations.

Persian vanilla cupcakes

MAKES 12

1. Preheat the oven to 320°F/160°C. Line a 12-cupcake pan with cupcake papers. In a medium-sized bowl, lightly beat the eggs, add butter and sugar, then mix until light and fluffy.
2. Add milk, flour and vanilla, and stir to combine. Beat with an electric mixer for 2 minutes, until light and creamy.
3. Divide the mixture evenly between the cake papers. Bake for 18–20 minutes until risen and firm to touch. Allow to cool for a few minutes and then transfer to a wire rack. Allow to cool fully before icing.

TOPPING

1. Meanwhile, combine all topping ingredients except fairy floss, mix with a wooden spoon until well combined, and beat with the spoon until light and fluffy.
2. Place mixture into a piping bag with a star-shaped nozzle and pipe onto all cupcakes. Top with fairy floss.

3 eggs
½ cup butter, softened
1 cup superfine/caster sugar
½ cup milk
1½ cups bakers/self-raising flour, sifted
1 teaspoon vanilla extract

TOPPING
1½ cup confectioners'/icing sugar
1 teaspoon lemon extract
1 teaspoon vanilla extract
½ cup butter, softened
Persian fairy floss (available from Middle Eastern grocers)

Marshmallow vanilla buttercups

MAKES 12

3 eggs
½ cup butter, softened
1 cup superfine/caster sugar
½ cup buttermilk
1½ cups bakers/self-raising flour,
*   sifted*
2 teaspoons vanilla extract

TOPPING
3½ oz/100g confectioners'/icing
*   sugar*
½ cup butter, softened
1 teaspoon vanilla extract
marshmallow dots (3½ oz/100g
*   minimum)*

1. Preheat the oven to 320°F/160°C. Line a 12-cupcake pan with cupcake papers. In a medium-sized bowl, lightly beat the eggs, add butter and sugar, then mix until light and fluffy.
2. Add buttermilk, flour and vanilla, and stir to combine. Beat with an electric mixer for 2 minutes, until light and creamy.
3. Divide the mixture evenly between the cake papers. Bake for 18–20 minutes until risen and firm to touch. Allow to cool for a few minutes and then transfer to a wire rack. Allow to cool fully before icing.

TOPPING
1. Meanwhile, combine half the sugar and butter, mix with a wooden spoon, add remaining sugar, butter and vanilla extract and beat with the spoon until light and fluffy.
2. Add dollop (tablespoon-sized) of topping to the centre of each cake. Make a flower design with the small marshmallows in the centre of each cupcake.

Buttermilk bootie cupcakes

MAKES 12

1. Preheat the oven to 320°F/160°C. Line a 12-cupcake pan with cupcake papers. In a medium-sized bowl, lightly beat the eggs, add butter and sugar, then mix until light and fluffy.
2. Add milk, flour and vanilla, and stir to combine. Beat with an electric mixer for 2 minutes, until light and creamy.
3. Divide the mixture evenly between the cake papers. Bake for 18–20 minutes until risen and firm to touch. Allow to cool for a few minutes and then transfer to a wire rack. Allow to cool fully before icing.

TOPPING
1. Meanwhile, combine half the sugar and butter, mix with a wooden spoon, add the remaining sugar and butter and beat with the spoon until light and fluffy.
2. Divide the topping into two bowls, and add blue food colouring to one and pink to the other. Spread the topping evenly onto the cupcakes and then top with baby booties.

3 eggs
½ cup butter, softened
1 cup superfine/caster sugar
½ cup milk
1½ cups bakers/self-raising flour, sifted
1 teaspoon vanilla extract

TOPPING
1½ cups confectioners'/icing sugar
½ cup butter, softened
blue and pink food colouring
baby booties (available from specialty cake decoration stores)

Vanilla rose cupcakes

MAKES 12

3 eggs
½ cup butter, softened
1 cup superfine/caster sugar
½ cup milk
1½ cups bakers/self-raising flour,
    sifted
1 teaspoon vanilla extract

TOPPING
1½ cups confectioners'/icing
    sugar
1 teaspoon rose water
½ cup butter, softened
6 drops vanilla extract
miniature dried roses,
    approximately 8 per cupcake
    (available from specialty cake
    decoration stores)

1. Preheat the oven to 320°F/160°C. Line a 12-cupcake pan with cupcake papers. In a medium-sized bowl, lightly beat the eggs, add butter and sugar, then mix until light and fluffy.

2. Add milk, flour and vanilla, and stir to combine. Beat with an electric mixer for 2 minutes, until light and creamy.

3. Divide the mixture evenly between the cake papers. Bake for 18–20 minutes until risen and firm to touch. Allow to cool for a few minutes and then transfer to a wire rack. Allow to cool fully before icing.

TOPPING
1. Meanwhile, combine half of all the topping ingredients except roses, mix with a wooden spoon, add remaining ingredients and beat with the spoon until light and fluffy. Place mixture into a piping bag with a plain nozzle and pipe onto cupcakes. Decorate with roses.

Lavender buttercream cupcakes

MAKES 12

1. Preheat the oven to 320°F/160°C. Line a 12-cupcake pan with cupcake papers. In a medium-sized bowl, lightly beat the eggs, add butter and sugar, then mix until light and fluffy.
2. Add milk, flour and vanilla, and stir to combine. Beat with an electric mixer for 2 minutes, until light and creamy.
3. Divide the mixture evenly between the cake papers. Bake for 18–20 minutes until risen and firm to touch. Allow to cool for a few minutes and then transfer to a wire rack. Allow to cool fully before icing.

TOPPING

1. Meanwhile, combine half the topping ingredients except candied lavender, mix with a wooden spoon, add remaining ingredients and beat with a whisk until light and fluffy.
2. Apply the topping with the back of a teaspoon or a small spatula. Place the candied lavender on top.

3 eggs
½ cup butter, softened
1 cup superfine/caster sugar
½ cup milk
1½ cups bakers/self-raising flour, sifted
1 teaspoon vanilla extract

TOPPING
1½ cups confectioners'/icing sugar
1 teaspoon lavender extract
½ cup butter, softened
2 drops purple food colouring
candied lavender (available from cake decoration stores)

Vanilla heart cupcakes

MAKES 12

3 eggs
½ cup butter, softened
1 cup superfine/caster sugar
½ cup milk
1½ cups bakers/self-raising flour,
  sifted
1 teaspoon vanilla extract
3½ oz/100g white chocolate,
  chopped

TOPPING
⅓ cup confectioners'/icing sugar
2 tablespoons water
⅓ cup seedless strawberry jam
12 heart-shaped candles

1. Preheat the oven to 320°F/160°C.
   Line a 12-cupcake pan with cupcake
   papers. In a medium-sized bowl, lightly
   beat the eggs, add butter and sugar,
   then mix until light and fluffy.

2. Add milk, flour and vanilla, and stir to
   combine. Beat with an electric mixer
   for 2 minutes, until light and creamy.
   Add white chocolate and stir through
   the mixture.

3. Divide the mixture evenly between the
   cake papers. Bake for 18–20 minutes
   until risen and firm to touch. Allow to
   cool for a few minutes and then transfer
   to a wire rack. Allow to cool fully before
   icing.

TOPPING
1. Meanwhile, combine confectioners'
   sugar and water in a small bowl. Add
   strawberry jam to a piping bag using
   the smallest nozzle, and pipe over the
   cake. Repeat with white icing. Top with
   a heart-shaped candle.

White musk cupcakes

MAKES 12

1. Preheat the oven to 320°F/160°C. Line a 12-cupcake pan with cupcake papers. In a medium-sized bowl, lightly beat the eggs, add butter and sugar, and mix until light and fluffy.
2. Add milk, flour, vanilla and rose water, and stir to combine. Beat with an electric mixer for 2 minutes, until light and creamy.
3. Divide the mixture evenly between the cake papers. Bake for 18–20 minutes until risen and firm to touch. Allow to cool for a few minutes and then transfer to a wire rack. Allow to cool fully before icing.

TOPPING

1. Meanwhile, combine all the topping ingredients except musk stick pieces in a small bowl, mix with a wooden spoon until well combined, then whisk until light and fluffy.
2. Place mixture into a piping bag with a star-shaped nozzle and pipe onto all cupcakes. Top with musk stick slices.

3 eggs
½ cup butter, softened
1 cup superfine/caster sugar
½ cup milk
1½ cups bakers/self-raising flour, sifted
1 teaspoon vanilla extract
6 drops rose water

TOPPING
1½ cups confectioners'/icing sugar
½ cup butter, softened
6 drops rose water
small quantity of musk sticks, cut into slices

Triple white cupcakes

MAKES 12

3 eggs
½ cup butter, softened
1 cup superfine/caster sugar
½ cup milk
1½ cups bakers/self-raising flour,
  sifted
1 teaspoon vanilla extract
3½ oz/100g white chocolate,
  chopped

TOPPING
7 oz/200g white chocolate
  buttons
1 tablespoon butter, softened
⅓ cup cream, thickened
½ cup butter, softened
½ cup confectioners'/icing sugar

1. Preheat the oven to 320°F/160°C. Line a 12-cupcake pan with cupcake papers. In a medium-sized bowl, lightly beat the eggs, add butter and sugar, then mix until light and fluffy.

2. Add milk, flour and vanilla, and stir to combine. Beat with an electric mixer for 2 minutes, until light and creamy. Add white chocolate and stir through the mixture.

3. Divide the mixture evenly between the cake papers. Bake for 18–20 minutes until risen and firm to touch. Allow to cool for a few minutes and then transfer to a wire rack. Allow to cool fully before icing.

TOPPING

1. Meanwhile, combine 5½ oz/160g of the white chocolate with 1 tablespoon of butter in a medium-sized saucepan over a medium heat. As mixture begins to melt, add cream slowly, then reduce heat to low, stirring, until mixture thickens. Remove from heat and cool.

2. Combine butter and sugar, and mix with a wooden spoon. Beat with the spoon until light and fluffy. Add melted chocolate, combine, then spoon onto cupcakes. Top with remaining white chocolate buttons.

chocolate cupcakes

Chocolate is one of the great foods of modern celebration, whether it's in the form of a treat at a specialist chocolate store, a block of good chocolate bought at the supermarket after a hard day, or a chocolate dessert ordered at a birthday dinner out. This set of recipes will give you a whole new collection of ways to create chocolate treats for the whole family or for that weekend of indulgence.

Jaffa Ganache Cupcakes

Triple Choc Cupcakes

Chocolate Honeycomb Cupcakes

Butter Choc Cupcakes

Hazel Choc Cupcakes

Choc Chip Cupcakes

Vanilla Choc Cupcakes

Chocky Road Cupcakes

Persian Chocolate Cupcakes

Chili Choc Cupcakes

Almond Choc Cupcakes

Jaffa ganache cupcakes

MAKES 12

3 eggs
½ cup butter, softened
1 cup superfine/caster sugar
½ cup milk
1½ cups bakers/self-raising flour,
  sifted
1 teaspoon vanilla extract
3½ oz/100g dark chocolate
  pieces
1 tablespoon cocoa powder
1 teaspoon orange essence

TOPPING
3½ oz/100g dark chocolate,
  grated
¾ oz/20g butter, softened
⅓ cup thickened cream
1 teaspoon orange essence
1 piece candied orange, cut into
  slivers

1. Preheat the oven to 320°F/160°C.
   Line a 12-cupcake pan with cupcake
   papers. In a medium-sized bowl, lightly
   beat the eggs, add butter and sugar,
   then mix until light and fluffy.
2. Add milk, flour and vanilla, and stir to
   combine. Add remaining ingredients.
   Beat with an electric mixer for 2
   minutes, until light and creamy.
3. Divide the mixture evenly between the
   cake papers. Bake for 18–20 minutes
   until risen and firm to touch. Allow to cool
   for a few minutes and then transfer to a
   wire rack. Allow to cool fully before icing.

TOPPING
1. Meanwhile, combine the chocolate and
   butter in a medium-sized saucepan
   over a medium heat. As the mixture
   begins to melt, reduce heat to low,
   stirring constantly, until melted. Remove
   from heat, add cream and orange
   essence, and stir. Rest for 10 minutes:
   the mixture will be firm and velvety in
   consistency. Once cool, put in a piping
   bag with a small plain nozzle.
2. Pipe topping onto cupcakes in a spiral
   and top with candied orange pieces.

Triple choc cupcakes

MAKES 12

1. Preheat the oven to 320°F/160°C. Line a 12-cupcake pan with cupcake papers. In a medium-sized bowl, lightly beat the eggs, add butter and sugar, then mix until light and fluffy.
2. Add milk and flour, and stir to combine. Add the dark chocolate and cocoa powder, and stir through mixture. Beat with an electric mixer for 2 minutes, until light and creamy.
3. Divide the mixture evenly between the cupcake papers. Bake for 18–20 minutes until risen and firm to touch. Allow to cool for a few minutes and then transfer to a wire rack. Allow to cool fully before icing.

TOPPING

1. Meanwhile, combine the chocolate and butter in a medium-sized saucepan over a medium heat. As the mixture begins to melt, reduce heat to low, stirring constantly, until melted. Remove from heat, add cream, cocoa powder and sugar, and stir to combine. Rest for 10 minutes: the mixture will be firm and velvety in consistency. Use the back of a spoon to apply icing to cupcake.

3 eggs
½ cup butter, softened
1 cup superfine/caster sugar
½ cup milk
1½ cups bakers/self-raising flour, sifted
3½ oz/100g dark chocolate pieces
1 tablespoon cocoa powder

TOPPING
3½ oz/100g dark chocolate, chopped
¾ oz/20g butter, softened
⅓ cup thickened cream
2 tablespoons cocoa powder
1 teaspoon confectioners'/icing sugar

Chocolate honeycomb cupcakes

MAKES 12

3 eggs
½ cup butter, softened
1 cup superfine/caster sugar
½ cup buttermilk
1½ cups bakers/self-raising flour, sifted
1 teaspoon vanilla extract

TOPPING
½ cup chocolate drops
½ cup butter, softened
⅓ cup thickened cream
1½ cups confectioners'/icing sugar
1 teaspoon vanilla extract
½ cup pre-made honeycomb pieces, crumbled

1. Preheat oven to 320°F/160°C. Line a 12-cupcake pan with cupcake papers. In a medium-sized bowl, lightly beat eggs, add butter and sugar, then mix until light and fluffy.
2. Add buttermilk, flour and vanilla, and stir to combine. Beat with an electric mixer for 2 minutes, until light and creamy.
3. Divide mixture evenly between cupcake papers. Bake for 18–20 minutes until risen and firm to touch. Allow to cool for a few minutes and then transfer to a wire rack. Allow to cool fully before icing.

TOPPING
1. Meanwhile, combine chocolate and half the butter in a medium-sized saucepan over a medium heat. As mixture begins to melt, reduce heat to low, stirring constantly, until melted. Remove from heat, add cream, and stir. Rest for 10 minutes: the mixture will be firm and velvety in consistency.
2. Combine remaining butter, sugar and vanilla extract, and stir until light and fluffy. Add melted chocolate mixture, and stir to combine. Apply icing to each cupcake with a knife. Top each cupcake with a cluster of crumbled honeycomb.

Butter choc cupcakes

MAKES 12

1. Preheat the oven to 320°F/160°C. Line a 12-cupcake pan with cupcake papers. In a medium-sized bowl, lightly beat the eggs, add butter and sugar, then mix until light and fluffy.
2. Add buttermilk, flour, cocoa powder and vanilla, and stir to combine. Beat with an electric mixer for 2 minutes, until light and creamy. Add chocolate and cream, stir mixture thoroughly.
3. Divide the mixture evenly between the cake papers. Bake for 18–20 minutes until risen and firm to touch. Allow to cool for a few minutes and then transfer to a wire rack. Allow to cool fully before icing.

TOPPING

1. Meanwhile, combine half the sugar and butter, mix with a wooden spoon, add remaining sugar, butter and food colouring and beat with the spoon until light and fluffy. Add icing to a piping bag and pipe onto cupcakes, then smooth over with spatula and top with flower decorations.

3 eggs
½ cup butter, softened
1 cup superfine/caster sugar
½ cup buttermilk
1½ cups bakers/self-raising flour, sifted
1 teaspoon cocoa powder
1 teaspoon vanilla extract
½ cup milk chocolate pieces, finely chopped
⅓ cup pure cream

TOPPING
1½ cups cup confectioners'/icing sugar
½ cup butter, softened
5 drops pink food colouring
sugar flowers (available from good supermarkets and cake decoration shops)

Hazel choc cupcakes

MAKES 12

3 eggs
½ cup butter, softened
1 cup superfine/caster sugar
½ cup milk
1½ cups bakers/self-raising flour, sifted
1 teaspoon vanilla extract
3½ oz/100g dark chocolate pieces
1 tablespoon cocoa powder

TOPPING
3½ oz/100g dark chocolate pieces
1 tablespoon butter, softened
⅓ cup cream,thickened
½ cup butter, softened
½ cup confectioners'/icing sugar
3½ oz/100g hazelnuts

1. Preheat the oven to 320°F/160°C. Line a 12-cupcake pan with cupcake papers. In a medium-sized bowl, lightly beat the eggs, add butter and sugar, then mix until light and fluffy.
2. Add milk, flour and vanilla, and stir to combine. Add remaining ingredients. Beat with an electric mixer for 2 minutes, until light and creamy.
3. Divide the mixture evenly between the cake papers. Bake for 18–20 minutes until risen and firm to touch. Allow to cool for a few minutes and then transfer to a wire rack. Allow to cool fully before icing.

TOPPING
1. Meanwhile, combine the chocolate and 1 tablespoon of butter in a medium-sized saucepan over a medium heat. As the mixture begins to melt, add cream slowly, then reduce heat to low, stirring constantly, until mixture thickens. Remove from heat and cool.
2. Combine butter and sugar, and mix with wooden spoon. Beat with the spoon until light and fluffy. Add melted chocolate and half of the hazelnuts, combine, and then spoon onto cupcakes. Top with the remaining nuts.

Choc chip cupcakes

MAKES 12

1. Preheat oven to 320°F/160°C. Line a 12-cupcake pan with cupcake papers. In a medium-sized bowl, lightly beat the eggs, add butter and sugar, then mix until light and fluffy.
2. Beat with an electric mixer for 2 minutes, until light and creamy. Add milk, flour and vanilla, and stir to combine. Add milk chocolate and cocoa powder. Stir through mixture.
3. Divide mixture evenly between cupcake papers. Bake for 18–20 minutes until risen and firm to touch. Allow to cool for a few minutes and then transfer to a wire rack. Allow to cool fully before icing.

TOPPING

1. Meanwhile, combine chocolate and half of butter in a medium-sized saucepan over a medium heat. As mixture begins to melt, reduce heat to low, stirring until melted. Remove from heat, add cream, and stir. Rest for 10 minutes: the mixture will be firm and velvety in consistency.
2. Combine remaining butter, sugar and vanilla extract, stir until light and fluffy. Add melted chocolate mixture, stir in chocolate drops, spoon onto cupcakes. Sprinkle with small chocolate drops.

3 eggs
½ cup butter, softened
1 cup superfine/caster sugar
½ cup milk
1½ cups bakers/self-raising flour, sifted
1 teaspoon vanilla extract
½ cup milk chocolate drops
1 tablespoon cocoa powder

TOPPING
½ cup milk chocolate, grated
1½ cups butter, softened
⅓ cup thickened cream
½ cup confectioners'/icing sugar
1 teaspoon vanilla extract
½ cup milk chocolate drops
½ cup small choc drops

Vanilla choc cupcakes

MAKES 12

3 eggs
½ cup butter, softened
1 cup superfine/caster sugar
½ cup vanilla-flavoured yoghurt
1½ cups bakers/self-raising flour,
  sifted
1 tablespoon vanilla extract
3½ oz/100g dark chocolate
  pieces
1 tablespoon cocoa powder

TOPPING
3½ oz/100g dark chocolate
  pieces
¾ oz/20g butter, softened
⅓ cup thickened cream
silver cachous (available from
  cake decoration stores and
  supermarkets)

1. Preheat the oven to 320°F/160°C. Line a 12-cupcake pan with cupcake papers. In a medium-sized bowl, lightly beat the eggs, add butter and sugar, then mix until light and fluffy.
2. Add yoghurt, flour and vanilla, and stir to combine. Add remaining ingredients. Beat with an electric mixer for 2 minutes, until light and creamy.
3. Divide the mixture evenly between the cake papers. Bake for 18–20 minutes until risen and firm to touch. Allow to cool for a few minutes, and then transfer to a wire rack. Allow to cool fully before icing.

TOPPING

1. Meanwhile, combine the chocolate and butter in a medium-sized saucepan over a medium heat. As the mixture begins to melt, reduce heat to low, stirring constantly, until melted. Remove from heat, add cream, and stir. Rest for 10 minutes: the mixture will be firm and velvety in consistency. Use a fork to apply icing to each cupcake, and add silver cachous to finish.

Chocky road cupcakes

MAKES 12

1. Preheat the oven to 320°F/160°C. Line a 12-cupcake pan with cupcake papers. In a medium-sized bowl, lightly beat the eggs, add butter and sugar, then mix until light and fluffy.
2. Add milk, flour, vanilla and cocoa powder, stir to combine. Beat with an electric mixer for 2 minutes, until light and creamy.
3. Divide the mixture evenly between the cupcake papers. Bake for 18–20 minutes until risen and firm to touch. Allow to cool for a few minutes and then transfer to a wire rack. Allow to cool fully before icing.

TOPPING

1. Meanwhile, combine chocolate and half of the butter in a medium-sized saucepan over a medium heat. As the mixture begins to melt, reduce heat to low, stirring until melted. Remove from heat, add cream, stir. Rest for 10 minutes: the mixture will be firm and velvety in consistency.
2. Combine remaining butter, sugar and vanilla extract, stir until light and fluffy. Add melted chocolate mixture, stir to combine. Ice the top of each cupcake and decorate with cherry, almond and marshmallow.

3 eggs
½ cup butter, softened
1 cup superfine/caster sugar
½ cup milk
1½ cups bakers/self-raising flour, sifted
1 teaspoon vanilla extract
1 tablespoon cocoa powder

TOPPING
½ cup milk chocolate drops
½ cup butter, softened
⅓ cup thickened cream
1½ cups confectioners'/icing sugar
1 teaspoon vanilla extract
¼ cup glacé cherries, chopped
⅓ cup almonds, chopped
⅓ cup marshmallows, chopped

Persian chocolate cupcakes

MAKES 12

3 eggs
½ cup butter, softened
1 cup superfine/caster sugar
½ cup milk
1½ cups bakers/self-raising flour,
  sifted
1 teaspoon vanilla extract
3½ oz/100g dark chocolate
  pieces
1 tablespoon cocoa powder

TOPPING
1½ cups confectioners'/icing
  sugar
½ cup butter, softened
2 teaspoons cocoa powder
Persian fairy floss (available from
  Middle Eastern grocery stores)
1 tablespoon cocoa powder, for
  dusting

1. Preheat the oven to 320°F/160°C. Line a 12-cupcake pan with cupcake papers. In a medium-sized bowl, lightly beat the eggs, add butter and sugar, then mix until light and fluffy.
2. Add milk, flour and vanilla, and stir to combine. Add remaining ingredients. Beat with an electric mixer for 2 minutes, until light and creamy.
3. Divide the mixture evenly between the cake papers. Bake for 18–20 minutes until risen and firm to touch. Allow to cool for a few minutes and then transfer to a wire rack. Allow to cool fully before icing.

TOPPING
1. Meanwhile, combine half the sugar and butter, mix with a wooden spoon, add remaining sugar, butter and cocoa powder and beat with the spoon until light and fluffy.
2. Add icing to a piping bag with a small nozzle and pipe onto cupcakes in a spiral. Top with Persian fairy floss and a dusting of cocoa.

Chili choc cupcakes

MAKES 12

1. Preheat the oven to 320°F/160°C. Line a 12-cupcake pan with cupcake papers. Slice chilies in half and remove seeds – place chilies in a cup with ¼ cup of hot water to soak for 10 minutes. In a medium-sized bowl, lightly beat the eggs, add butter and sugar, then mix until light and fluffy.
2. Add milk, flour and vanilla, and stir to combine. Add chocolate, cocoa powder and half chili-infused water, and combine. Beat with an electric mixer for 2 minutes, until light and creamy.
3. Divide mixture evenly between cake papers. Bake for 18–20 minutes until risen and firm to touch. Cool, transfer to a wire rack. Cool fully before icing.

TOPPING

1. Meanwhile, combine the chocolate and butter in a medium-sized saucepan over a medium heat. As the mixture begins to melt, reduce heat to low, stirring until melted. Remove from heat, add cream and remaining chili water and stir. Rest for 10 minutes: the mixture will be firm and velvety in consistency. Put in a piping bag with a small plain nozzle and pipe onto cakes. Top with fresh small chilies.

2 small fresh chilies or
1 teaspoon dry red chili flakes
3 eggs
½ cup butter, softened
1 cup superfine/caster sugar
½ cup milk
1½ cups bakers/self-raising flour, sifted
1 teaspoon vanilla extract
3½ oz/100g dark chocolate pieces
1 tablespoon cocoa powder

TOPPING
3½ oz/100g dark chocolate, chopped
¾ oz/20g butter, softened
⅓ cup thickened cream
remaining chili-infused water
chilies for decoration

Almond choc cupcakes

MAKES 12

3 eggs
½ cup butter, softened
1 cup superfine/caster sugar
½ cup milk
1½ cups bakers/self-raising flour,
  sifted
1 teaspoon vanilla extract
1 tablespoon cocoa powder

TOPPING
½ cup superfine/caster sugar, for
  toffee
3½ oz/100g dark chocolate
¾ oz/20g butter, softened
⅓ cup thickened cream
1 cup confectioners'/icing sugar
1 tablespoon cocoa powder
½ cup dark chocolate
3½ oz/100g almond flakes

1. Preheat the oven to 320°F/160°C. Line a 12-cupcake pan with cupcake papers. In a medium-sized bowl, lightly beat the eggs, add butter and sugar, then mix until light and fluffy.

2. Add milk, flour, vanilla and cocoa powder, and stir to combine. Beat with an electric mixer for 2 minutes, until light and creamy.

3. Divide mixture between cupcake papers. Bake for 18–20 minutes until risen and firm to touch. Allow to cool, transfer to a wire rack. Cool fully before icing.

TOPPING

1. Combine chocolate and butter in a medium-sized saucepan over medium heat. As mixture melts, reduce heat, stir until melted. Remove from heat, add cream, stir. Rest for 10 minutes: mixture will be firm and velvety in consistency.

2. Combine sugar and cocoa powder, stir with wooden spoon until mixed together, then beat with spoon until light and fluffy. Add chocolate mixture and mix with a wooden spoon until light and fluffy. Spread evenly onto cupcakes with a teaspoon or spatula. Decorate with almond and broken toffee pieces.

coffee cupcakes

Coffee is the perfect accompaniment for cupcakes. Why not double up on taste and put a little coffee into your cupcakes? These caffeine-laced delicacies will make a great addition to a mid-afternoon pick-me-up, whether on the weekend with the colour supplement from your favourite newspaper in hand, or in your work lunchbox.

Coffee Muds

Coffee Raisin Cupcakes

Cappuccino Top Cupcakes

Cappuccino Cupcakes

Mocha Cupcakes

Irish Coffee Cupcakes

Pecan Coffee Crunch Cupcakes

Caffè Latte Cupcakes

Café Calypso Cupcakes

Long Black Cupcakes

Long Macchiato Cupcakes

Coffee muds

MAKES 12

8 oz/225g chocolate digestive
  biscuits
8 oz/225g butter, softened
8 oz/225g dark chocolate
1/3 cup golden syrup
3 medium eggs, beaten
1/2 teaspoon vanilla extract
1 tablespoon instant coffee

TOPPING
1¾ oz/50g white chocolate

1. Preheat the oven to 350°F/180°C. Line a 12-cupcake pan with cupcake papers. Place the biscuits into a plastic bag, seal, then crush with a rolling pin. Melt 2½ oz/75g of the butter in a saucepan. Remove from the heat and mix in the biscuits. Divide the biscuit mixture between the papers, pressing over the base and gently up the sides of each paper. Refrigerate for 20 minutes or until firm.

2. Put the remaining butter, chocolate and syrup into a double boiler. Heat gently, stirring, until melted. Remove from the heat and cool for 5 minutes. Whisk in the eggs, vanilla extract and coffee.

3. Spoon the chocolate mixture over the biscuit bases and bake for 20 minutes or until just firm. Leave to cool for 5 minutes.

TOPPING

1. Meanwhile, melt the white chocolate in a double boiler. Drizzle over the cakes.

Coffee raisin cupcakes

MAKES 24

1. Preheat the oven to 400°F/200°C. Set out 24 mini-cupcake papers on a baking sheet.
2. Stir together the flour and baking powder in a medium-sized bowl. Stir in the raisins. Beat the butter, sugar, and 2 teaspoons of the coffee in a large bowl until creamy. Add the eggs, one at a time, until just blended. Fold in the dry ingredients.
3. Divide the mixture evenly between the cupcake papers. Bake for 12–15 minutes until risen and firm to touch. Allow to cool for a few minutes and then transfer to a wire rack. Allow to cool fully before icing.

TOPPING
1. Combine the sugar and remaining coffee, and mix with enough water to make a soft icing. Apply icing to each cupcake with a knife.

3½ oz/100g plain flour
1 teaspoon baking powder
¼ cup raisins
½ cup butter, softened
½ cup superfine/caster sugar
1 tablespoon instant coffee
2 eggs

TOPPING
½ cup confectioners'/icing sugar
2–3 tablespoons boiling water

Cappuccino top cupcakes

10½ oz/300g butter, softened
12 egg whites
2¼ cups all-purpose/plain flour
¾ cup coffee beans, very finely
 ground
3 cups confectioners'/icing sugar
½ teaspoon allspice

TOPPING
3 egg whites
¾ cup superfine/caster sugar
2 teaspoons raw sugar, for
 decorating

1. Preheat the oven to 350°F/180°C. Line a 12-cupcake pan with cupcake papers. Heat butter in a saucepan until it turns golden, then remove from heat.
2. Beat the 12 egg whites until soft peaks form, then fold in flour, coffee, sugar and allspice. Pour in butter and fold to combine.
3. Divide the mixture evenly between the cake papers. Spoon topping over cake batter.
4. Bake for 15–20 minutes until cakes are cooked and meringue is lightly golden. Sprinkle with raw sugar to serve.

TOPPING
1. For the topping, beat egg whites until frothy, then beat in sugar until thick and glossy.

Cappuccino cupcakes

MAKES 12

1. Preheat the oven to 350°F/180°C. Line a 12-cupcake pan with cupcake papers. In a saucepan, heat the butter, milk and coffee gently and stir until butter is melted. Allow to cool.
2. In a large bowl, whisk the eggs with an electric mixer until thick and creamy. Add the sugar gradually, then stir in half the butter mixture and flour and beat. Add the remaining butter mixture and flour and beat until smooth.
3. Divide the mixture evenly between the cake papers. Bake for 20 minutes until risen and firm to touch. Allow to cool for a few minutes and then transfer to a wire rack. Allow to cool fully before icing.

TOPPING

1. Meanwhile, combine all of the ingredients in a medium-sized bowl and beat slowly with an electric mixer to combine for 1 minute. Turn speed up and beat until combined. Place mixture into a piping bag and pipe onto all cupcakes. Dust with sugar and cocoa powder.

9 oz/250g butter, softened
1½ cups milk
1 tablespoon instant coffee
6 eggs
2 cups superfine/caster sugar
3 cups bakers/self-raising flour

TOPPING
3 cups confectioners'/icing sugar
1 cup milk powder
2 tablespoons instant coffee
3½ oz/100g butter, softened
¼ cup milk
4 drops vanilla extract
confectioners'/icing sugar and
    cocoa powder, for dusting

Mocha cupcakes

MAKES 12

3 eggs
½ cup butter, softened
1 cup superfine/caster sugar
½ cup milk
1 cup bakers/self-raising flour,
    sifted
¼ teaspoon baking powder
½ cup hazelnut meal
½ cup hazelnuts, chopped
¼ cup cocoa powder
3 tablespoons instant coffee

TOPPING
1 cup confectioners'/icing sugar
½ cup unsalted butter, softened
1 tablespoon hazelnut liqueur
1 teaspoon instant coffee
36 coffee beans

1. Preheat the oven to 320°F/160°C. Line a 12-cupcake pan with cupcake papers. In a medium-sized bowl, lightly beat the eggs, add butter and sugar, then mix until light and fluffy.
2. Add milk and flour, and stir to combine. Add remaining cake ingredients. Mix with a wooden spoon for 2 minutes, until light and creamy.
3. Divide the mixture evenly between the cake papers. Bake for 18–20 minutes until risen and firm to touch. Allow to cool for a few minutes, and then transfer to a wire rack. Allow to cool fully before icing.

TOPPING
1. Meanwhile, combine all topping ingredients except for coffee beans in a small bowl, mix with a wooden spoon, and spoon onto cupcakes. Decorate each cake with a few coffee beans.

Irish coffee cupcakes

MAKES 12

1. Preheat the oven to 350°/180°C. Line a 12-cupcake pan with cupcake papers. In a saucepan, heat the butter, milk, milk powder and coffee gently and stir until butter is melted. Allow to cool.
2. In a large bowl, whisk the eggs with an electric mixer until thick and creamy. Add the sugar gradually, then stir in half the butter mixture and flour and beat. Add the whiskey and the remaining butter mixture and flour and beat until smooth.
3. Divide the mixture evenly between the cake papers. Bake for 20 minutes until risen and firm to touch. Allow to cool for a few minutes and then transfer to a wire rack. Allow to cool fully before icing.

TOPPING

1. Meanwhile, combine all of the ingredients except the whiskey and shamrocks in a medium-sized bowl and beat with an electric mixer to slowly combine for 1 minute. Turn speed up and beat until combined. Add the whiskey slowly and mix again until thoroughly combined. Place mixture into a piping bag and pipe onto all cupcakes. Sprinkle with the shamrocks.

9 oz/250g butter, softened
1 cup milk
½ tablespoon milk powder
1½ tablespoons instant coffee
6 eggs
2 cups superfine/caster sugar
3 cups bakers/self-raising flour
½ cup Irish whiskey

TOPPING

3 cups confectioners'/icing sugar
1¼ cups milk powder
3½ oz/100g butter, softened
¼ cup milk
1 tablespoon Irish whiskey
shamrock candy decorations
(available from cake decoration stores)

Pecan coffee crunch cupcakes

MAKES 12

3 eggs
½ cup butter, softened
1 cup superfine/caster sugar
¼ cup milk
1½ cups bakers/self-raising flour,
  sifted
1 tablespoon espresso coffee
½ cup pecans, chopped
1 tablespoon golden syrup

TOPPING
1 cup packed brown sugar
⅓ cup unsalted butter, softened
⅔ fl oz/20ml water
1 teaspoon vanilla extract
3½ oz/100g pecans

1. Preheat the oven to 320°F/160°C. Line
   a 12-cupcake pan with cupcake
   papers. In a medium-sized bowl, lightly
   beat the eggs, add butter and sugar,
   then mix until light and fluffy.
2. Add milk and flour, and stir to combine.
   Add remaining ingredients. Mix with a
   wooden spoon for 2 minutes, until light
   and creamy.
3. Divide the mixture evenly between the
   cake papers. Bake for 18–20 minutes
   until risen and firm to touch. Allow to
   cool for a few minutes, then transfer to
   a wire rack. Allow to cool fully before
   icing.

TOPPING
1. Meanwhile, combine sugar, butter,
   water and vanilla in a saucepan. Bring
   to a simmer over medium–low heat,
   stirring constantly. Without stirring
   again, simmer 1 minute. Remove from
   heat, add pecans, allow to cool slightly
   and spoon onto cakes in mounds.

Caffè latte cupcakes

MAKES 12

1. Preheat the oven to 350°/180°C. Line a 12-cupcake pan with cupcake papers. In a saucepan, heat the butter, ¼ cup of milk and vanilla gently and stir until butter is melted. Add the remaining milk and allow to cool.

2. In a large bowl, whisk the eggs with an electric mixer until thick and creamy. Add the sugar gradually, then stir in half the butter mixture and flour and beat. Add the remaining butter mixture, flour, skim milk powder and coffee and beat until smooth.

3. Divide the mixture evenly between the cake papers. Bake for 20 minutes until risen and firm to touch. Allow to cool for a few minutes and then transfer to a wire rack. Allow to cool fully before icing.

TOPPING

1. Meanwhile, combine all of the ingredients in a medium-sized bowl and beat with an electric mixer to slowly combine for 1 minute. Turn speed up and beat for 5 minutes until combined. Place mixture into a piping bag and pipe onto all cupcakes.

4 oz/125g butter, softened
¾ cup milk, scalded then cooled
½ teaspoon vanilla extract
3 eggs
1 cup superfine/caster sugar
1½ cups bakers/self-raising flour
1½ tablespoons skim milk powder
1 tablespoon instant coffee

TOPPING

3 cups confectioners'/icing sugar
1 cup milk powder
1 tablespoon instant coffee
3½ oz/100g butter, softened
¼ cup milk
4 drops vanilla extract

Café calypso cupcakes

MAKES 12

9 oz/260g butter, softened
1 cup milk
2 tablespoons instant coffee
6 eggs
2 cups superfine/caster sugar
3 cups bakers/self-raising flour
½ cup dark rum

TOPPING

3 cups confectioners'/icing sugar
1 cup milk powder
1 tablespoon instant coffee
3½ oz/100g butter, softened
¼ cup milk
4 drops rum extract
¼ cup instant coffee, for dusting

1. Preheat the oven to 350°F/180°C. Line a 12-cupcake pan with cupcake papers. In a saucepan, heat the butter, milk and coffee gently and stir until butter is melted. Allow to cool.

2. In a large bowl, whisk the eggs with an electric mixer until thick and creamy. Add the sugar gradually, then stir in half the butter mixture and flour and beat. Add the rum and the remaining butter mixture and flour and beat until smooth.

3. Divide the mixture evenly between the cake papers. Bake for 20 minutes until risen and firm to touch. Allow to cool for a few minutes and then transfer to a wire rack. Allow to cool fully before icing.

TOPPING

1. Meanwhile, combine all of the ingredients except the coffee in a medium-sized bowl and beat with an electric mixer to slowly combine for 1 minute. Turn speed up and beat until combined. Place mixture into a piping bag and pipe onto all cupcakes. Dust with instant coffee.

Long black cupcakes

MAKES 12

1. Preheat the oven to 350°F/180°C. Line a 12-cupcake pan with cupcake papers. Sift the dry ingredients together.
2. In a medium-sized bowl, beat the butter, vanilla and sugar with an electric mixer until creamy. Add the eggs one at a time and beat until well combined.
3. Add the dry ingredients to the butter mixture and combine thoroughly, then slowly add the water and mix again.
4. Divide the mixture evenly between the cake papers. Bake for approximately 20 minutes until risen and firm to touch. Allow to cool for a few minutes and then transfer to a wire rack. Allow to cool fully before icing.

TOPPING

1. Meanwhile, heat the coffee and cream gently in a saucepan. Pour mixture over the chocolate to melt it, and stir thoroughly. Place mixture into a piping bag with a star-shaped nozzle and pipe onto all cupcakes.

1½ cups bakers/self-raising flour
¾ cup all-purpose/plain flour
¼ cup cocoa powder
¼ cup instant coffee
6 oz/185g butter, softened
½ teaspoon vanilla extract
1½ cups superfine/caster sugar
3 eggs
1 cup water

TOPPING
1 tablespoon instant coffee
7 fl oz/200ml cream
9 oz/250g dark chocolate, finely chopped

Long macchiato cupcakes

½ cup all-purpose/plain flour
1 cup bakers/self-raising flour
4½ tablespoons instant coffee
4 oz/125g butter, softened
¼ teaspoon vanilla extract
1 cup superfine/caster sugar
2 eggs
¾ cup water

TOPPING
3 cups confectioners'/icing sugar
1 cup milk powder
1 tablespoon instant coffee
3½ oz/100g butter, softened
¼ cup milk
4 drops vanilla extract

1. Preheat the oven to 350°F/180°C. Line a 12-cupcake pan with cupcake papers. Sift the dry ingredients together.

2. In a medium-sized bowl, beat the butter, vanilla and sugar with an electric mixer until creamy. Add the eggs one at a time and beat until well combined.

3. Add the dry ingredients to the butter mixture and combine thoroughly, then slowly add the water and mix again.

4. Divide the mixtrue evenly between the cake papers. Bake for approximately 20 minutes until risen and firm to touch. Allow to cool for a few minutes and then transfer to a wire rack. Allow to cool fully before icing.

TOPPING
1. Meanwhile, combine all of the ingredients except the instant coffee in a medium-sized bowl and beat with an electric mixer to slowly combine for 1 minute. Turn speed up and beat until combined. Add 1 teaspoon of water to the coffee and add to the topping, stirring only once. Spread topping evenly onto cupcakes with a teaspoon.

fruit cupcakes

Fruit cupcakes could be thought of as starting to stray into muffin territory, but for the non-purist, these tasty little paper-cased treats can be a healthier option than other cupcakes and transport well in a child's lunchbox. Whether you cook small pieces of fresh or dried fruit into the body of the cupcake or add a piece to the topping, fruit adds a little goodness to a treat for the kids.

Triple Berry Cupcakes

Passion Yoghurt Cupcakes

Black Forest Cupcakes

Poppy Lime Cupcakes

Strawberry Surprise Cupcakes

Apple and Cinnamon Cupcakes

Cherry Choc Cupcakes

Banana Nut Cupcakes

Blue Bell Cupcakes

Orange Poppy Cupcakes

Peachy Piece Cupcakes

Triple berry cupcakes

MAKES 12

3 eggs
½ cup butter, softened
1 cup superfine/caster sugar
½ cup milk
2 tablespoons raspberry liqueur
1½ cups bakers/self-raising flour,
  sifted

TOPPING
½ cup confectioners'/icing sugar
2 tablespoons water
½ punnet strawberries
½ punnet blueberries
½ punnet blackberries

1. Preheat the oven to 320°F/160°C. Line a 12-cupcake pan with cupcake papers. In a medium-sized bowl, lightly beat the eggs, add butter and sugar, then mix until light and fluffy.

2. Add milk, liqueur and flour, and stir to combine. Beat with an electric mixer for 2 minutes, until light and creamy.

3. Divide the mixture evenly between the cake papers. Bake for 18–20 minutes until risen and firm to touch. Allow to cool for a few minutes and then transfer to a wire rack. Allow to cool fully before icing.

TOPPING

1. Meanwhile, combine sugar and water in a small bowl. Spoon a teaspoon of icing in the centre of each cupcake. Decorate with a cluster of fresh berries.

Passion yoghurt cupcakes

MAKES 12

1. Preheat the oven to 320°F/160°C. Line a 12-cupcake pan with cupcake papers. In a medium-sized bowl, lightly beat the eggs, add butter and sugar, then mix until light and fluffy.
2. Add yoghurt, flour and vanilla, and stir to combine. Beat with an electric mixer for 2 minutes, until light and creamy. Fold passionfruit pulp through mixture.
3. Divide the mixture evenly between the cake papers. Bake for 18–20 minutes until risen and firm to touch. Allow to cool for a few minutes and then transfer to a wire rack. Allow to cool fully before icing.

TOPPING

1. Meanwhile, combine sugar and yoghurt in a medium-sized bowl and mix with a wooden spoon. Add passionfruit pulp, mix to combine and spread topping on cupcakes.

3 eggs
1/2 cup butter, softened
1 cup superfine/caster sugar
1/2 cup plain yoghurt
1 1/2 cups bakers/self-raising flour, sifted
1 teaspoon vanilla extract
pulp 2 passionfruit

TOPPING
1 cup confectioners'/icing sugar
1/2 cup Greek-style yoghurt
pulp 1 passionfruit

Black forest cupcakes

MAKES 12

3 eggs
½ cup butter, softened
1 cup superfine/caster sugar
½ cup milk
1½ cups bakers/self-raising flour,
    sifted
¼ cup cocoa powder
1 tablespoon kirsch liqueur

TOPPING
3½ oz/100g cream
12 fresh cherries
¼ cup chocolate, shaved

1. Preheat the oven to 320°F/160°C. Line a 12-cupcake pan with cupcake papers. In a medium-sized bowl, lightly beat the eggs, add butter and sugar, then mix until light and fluffy.

2. Add milk, flour and cocoa powder, and stir to combine. Beat with an electric mixer for 2 minutes, until light and creamy, then fold through kirsch liqueur.

3. Divide the mixture evenly between the cake papers. Bake for 18–20 minutes until risen and firm to touch. Allow to cool for a few minutes and then transfer to a wire rack. Allow to cool fully before icing.

TOPPING

1. Meanwhile, whip cream until stiff peaks form, then top each cake with a dollop of cream, a sprinkle of chocolate shavings and a fresh cherry.

Poppy lime cupcakes

MAKES 12

1. Preheat the oven to 320°F/160°C. Line a 12-cupcake pan with cupcake papers. In a medium-sized bowl, lightly beat the eggs, add butter and sugar, then mix until light and fluffy.
2. Add yoghurt and flour, and stir to combine. Beat with an electric mixer for 2 minutes, until light and creamy. Add lime zest, lime juice and poppy seeds, and mix through with a wooden spoon.
3. Divide the mixture evenly between the cake cases. Bake for 18–20 minutes until risen and firm to touch. Allow to cool for a few minutes and then transfer to a wire rack. Allow to cool fully before icing.

TOPPING

1. Meanwhile, combine all the topping ingredients except the candied lime, mix with a wooden spoon, and spoon onto cakes. Top with candied lime pieces.

3 eggs
1/2 cup butter, softened
1 cup superfine/caster sugar
1/2 cup Greek-style yoghurt
1 1/2 cups bakers/self-raising flour, sifted
zest of 2 limes
juice of 1 lime
1 teaspoon poppy seeds

TOPPING
1 1/2 cups confectioners'/icing sugar
1/2 cup butter, softened
juice of 1 lime
1/2 teaspoon poppy seeds
zest of 1 lime
1 3/4 oz/50g candied lime, cut into thin slivers

Strawberry surprise cupcakes

MAKES 12

3 eggs
½ cup butter, softened
1 cup superfine/caster sugar
½ cup milk
1½ cups bakers/self-raising flour,
   sifted
2 tablespoons strawberry liqueur

TOPPING
1½ cups confectioners'/icing
   sugar
½ cup butter, softened
3 strawberries, quartered
strawberry-coloured flowers
   (available from cake decoration
   stores)

1. Preheat the oven to 320°F/160°C. Line a 12-cupcake pan with cupcake papers. In a medium-sized bowl, lightly beat the eggs, add butter and sugar, then mix until light and fluffy.

2. Add milk, flour and liqueur, and stir to combine. Beat with an electric mixer for 2 minutes, until light and creamy.

3. Divide the mixture evenly between the cake papers. Bake for 18–20 minutes until risen and firm to touch. Allow to cool for a few minutes and then transfer to a wire rack. Allow to cool fully before icing.

TOPPING

1. Meanwhile, combine sugar and butter in a small bowl, mix with a wooden spoon until well combined, then beat with a whisk until light and fluffy. Spoon mixture into a piping bag with a medium-sized star-shaped nozzle, and set aside.

2. With a sharp knife, slash the top of each cupcake and push a piece of strawberry into the centre. Pipe icing onto each cupcake and decorate with the red sugar flowers. Serve immediately.

Apple and cinnamon cupcakes

MAKES 12

1. Preheat the oven to 320°F/160°C. Line a 12-cupcake pan with cupcake papers.In a small bowl, coat the apple pieces with lemon juice and sprinkle with cinnamon. In a medium-sized bowl, lightly beat the eggs, add butter and sugar, then mix until light and fluffy.
2. Add milk and flour, and stir to combine. Beat with an electric mixer for 2 minutes, until light and creamy. Add spiced apple and stir through mixture.
3. Divide the mixture evenly between the cake papers. Bake for 18–20 minutes until risen and firm to touch. Allow to cool for a few minutes and then transfer to a wire rack. Allow to cool fully before icing.

TOPPING

1. Meanwhile, combine half the sugar and butter, mix with a wooden spoon, add remaining sugar and butter and beat with the spoon until light and fluffy. Spoon topping onto cupcakes and sprinkle cinnamon sugar on top.

½ apple, peeled and chopped
   into small pieces
juice of 1 lemon
1 tablespoon cinnamon
3 eggs
½ cup butter, softened
1 cup superfine/caster sugar
½ cup milk
1½ cups bakers/self-raising flour,
   sifted

TOPPING
1½ cups confectioners'/icing
   sugar
½ cup butter, softened
1 tablespoon cinnamon sugar

Cherry choc cupcakes

MAKES 12

3 eggs
1/2 cup butter, softened
1 cup superfine/caster sugar
1/2 cup milk
1 tablespoon kirsch liqueur
1 1/2 cups bakers/self-raising flour, sifted
7 oz/200g white chocolate, chopped

TOPPING
3 1/2 oz/100g white chocolate, chopped
1 tablespoon butter
1/3 cup thickened cream
1 tablespoon cherry liqueur
1/2 cup butter, softened
2/3 cup confectioners'/icing sugar
7 oz/200g glacé cherries, chopped

1. Preheat the oven to 320°F/160°C. Line a 12-cupcake pan with cupcake papers. In a medium-sized bowl, lightly beat the eggs, add butter and sugar, then mix until light and fluffy.

2. Add milk, liqueur and flour, and stir to combine. Beat with an electric mixer for 2 minutes, until light and creamy. Add white chocolate, and stir through mixture.

3. Divide the mixture evenly between the cake papers. Bake for 18–20 minutes until risen and firm to touch. Allow to cool for a few minutes and then transfer to a wire rack. Allow to cool fully before icing.

TOPPING

1. Meanwhile, combine the chocolate and tablespoon of butter in a medium-sized saucepan over a medium heat. As the mixture begins to melt, add cream and liqueur slowly, then reduce heat to low, stirring constantly until mixture thickens. Remove from heat and cool.

2. Combine butter and sugar, and mix with a wooden spoon. Beat with the spoon until light and fluffy. Add melted chocolate mixture and glacé cherries, stir until combined, and then spoon onto cupcakes.

Banana nut cupcakes

MAKES 12

1. Preheat the oven to 320°F/160°C. Line a 12-cupcake pan with cupcake papers. In a medium-sized bowl, lightly beat the eggs, add butter and sugar, then mix until light and fluffy.
2. Add milk, flour and peanut butter, and stir to combine. Beat with an electric mixer for 2 minutes, until light and creamy. Add banana and stir through mix.
3. Divide the mixture evenly between the cake papers. Bake for 18–20 minutes until risen and firm to touch. Allow to cool for a few minutes and then transfer to a wire rack. Allow to cool fully before icing.

TOPPING

1. Place ½ cup superfine sugar evenly on a greaseproof paper–lined baking tray, and bake at 400°F/200°C for approximately 25 minutes until toffee consistency forms. Cool until hardened.
2. Meanwhile, combine half the sugar, butter and peanut butter, and mix with a wooden spoon. Add remaining sugar, butter and peanut butter and beat with the spoon until light and fluffy. Use the back of a spoon to ice cakes. Drizzle golden syrup onto cakes and top with toffee pieces.

3 eggs
½ cup butter, softened
1 cup superfine/caster sugar
½ cup milk
1½ cups bakers/self-raising flour, sifted
1 teaspoon smooth peanut butter
1 sugar banana, mashed

TOPPING

½ cup superfine/caster sugar, for toffee
½ cup superfine/caster sugar, for toffee
1½ cups confectioners'/icing sugar
½ cup butter, softened
2 tablespoons crunchy unsalted peanut butter
1 tablespoon golden syrup

Blue bell cupcakes

MAKES 12

3 eggs
½ cup butter, softened
1 cup superfine/caster sugar
½ cup milk
1½ cups bakers/self-raising flour,
  sifted
1 teaspoon vanilla extract
½ punnet blueberries, chopped
  in half

TOPPING
1 cup confectioners'/icing sugar
2 tablespoons of blueberries,
  mashed
½ punnet blueberries

1. Preheat the oven to 320°F/160°C. Line a 12-cupcake pan with cupcake papers. In a medium-sized bowl, lightly beat the eggs, add butter and sugar, then mix until light and fluffy.

2. Add milk, flour and vanilla, and stir to combine. Beat with an electric mixer for 2 minutes, until light and creamy. Add blueberries and stir through the mixture.

3. Divide the mixture evenly between the cake papers. Bake for 18–20 minutes until risen and firm to touch. Allow to cool for a few minutes and then transfer to a wire rack. Allow to cool fully before icing.

TOPPING

1. Meanwhile, combine sugar and mashed berries in a medium-sized bowl and mix with a wooden spoon. Use a spatula to apply icing to each cupcake and top with a blueberry.

Orange poppy cupcakes

MAKES 12

1. Preheat the oven to 320°F/160°C. Line a 12-cupcake pan with cupcake papers. In a medium-sized bowl, lightly beat the eggs, add butter and sugar, then mix until light and fluffy.
2. Add buttermilk and flour, and stir to combine. Beat with an electric mixer for 2 minutes, until light and creamy. Add orange zest, orange juice and poppy seeds, and mix through with a wooden spoon.
3. Divide the mixture evenly between the cake cases. Bake for 18–20 minutes until risen and firm to touch. Allow to cool for a few minutes and then transfer to a wire rack. Allow to cool fully before icing.

TOPPING

1. Meanwhile, combine topping ingredients except candied orange, and mix with a wooden spoon. Spoon onto cakes. Top with candied orange pieces.

3 eggs
½ cup butter, softened
1 cup superfine/caster sugar
½ cup buttermilk
1½ cups bakers/self-raising flour, sifted
zest of 1 orange
juice of ½ orange
1 teaspoon poppy seeds

TOPPING
1½ cups confectioners'/icing sugar
½ cup butter, softened
juice of ½ orange
½ teaspoon poppy seeds
zest of 1 orange
candied orange pieces, cut into thin slivers

Peachy piece cupcakes

MAKES 12

3 eggs
½ cup butter, softened
1 cup superfine/caster sugar
½ cup milk
1½ cups bakers/self-raising flour, sifted
2 tablespoons peach liqueur

TOPPING
1½ cups confectioners'/icing sugar
½ cup butter, softened
1 teaspoon peach extract
1 drop orange food colouring
1 drop red food colouring
peach-coloured sugar flowers (available from cake decoration stores)

1. Preheat the oven to 320°F/160°C. Line a 12-cupcake pan with cupcake papers. In a medium-sized bowl, lightly beat the eggs, add butter and sugar, then mix until light and fluffy.
2. Add milk, flour and peach liqueur, and stir to combine. Beat with an electric mixer for 5 minutes, until light and creamy.
3. Divide the mixture evenly between the cake cases. Bake for 18–20 minutes. Transfer to a wire rack. Allow to cool fully before icing.

TOPPING
1. Combine all ingredients except sugar flowers in a small bowl, mix with a wooden spoon, then whisk until light and fluffy. Place mixture into a piping bag and pipe dots onto all cupcakes. Top each dot with a flower.

citrus cupcakes

Sugar and citrus create a wonderful partnership. Sweetness can be one-dimensional, and the addition of something sharp cuts the sugary intensity.
The same can be said in reverse: the tartness and strong acidic qualities of citrus fruits often need a helping hand from something sweet to mellow into a delicious dessert. These two work beautifully in this chapter.

Lime Pistachio Cupcakes

Marmalade Pecan Cupcakes

Ginger Lime Cupcakes

Double Lemon Cupcakes

Lemon Toffee Cupcakes

Orange Choc Swirl Cupcakes

Lime and Pistachio Cupcakes

Lemon Sour Cream Butter Cupcakes

Jaffa Choc Cupcakes

St Clement's Cupcakes

Orange and Ginger Cupcakes

Lime pistachio cupcakes

MAKES 12

3 eggs
1 cup superfine/caster sugar
¾ cup vegetable oil
¼ cup lime juice
2¼ cups plain flour
1 teaspoon ground cinnamon
2½ teaspoons baking powder
½ teaspoon ground cloves
¾ cup grated courgette/zucchini
zest of 1 lime
½ cup pistachio pieces

TOPPING
5 oz/150g confectioners'/icing
   sugar
zest 1 lime
1 teaspoon lime juice
3 oz/90g butter, softened
½ cup pistachio pieces
1 drop green food colouring

1. Preheat the oven to 350°F/180°C. Line a 12-cupcake pan with cupcake papers. In a medium-sized bowl, beat eggs, sugar, oil, and lime juice with an electric mixer until thoroughly combined and creamy.

2. Sift all dry ingredients except pistachios into a bowl, then add to egg mixture. Beat mixture for five minutes, then add the zucchini and lime zest and stir to combine. Fold through pistachios.

3. Divide the mixture evenly between the cake cases. Bake for 20–25 minutes. Transfer to a wire rack. Allow to cool fully before icing.

TOPPING

1. Meanwhile, combine topping ingredients except the pistachios, and beat with an electric mixer for 5 minutes until creamy. Use a spatula to apply topping to each cupcake and top with pistachio pieces.

Marmalade pecan cupcakes

MAKES 12

1. Preheat the oven to 320°F/160°C. Line a 12-cupcake pan with cupcake papers. In a medium-sized bowl, lightly beat the eggs, add butter and sugar, then mix until light and fluffy.
2. Add milk, flour and cocoa powder, and stir to combine. Beat with an electric mixer for 2 minutes, until light and creamy. Add zest, juice and nuts, and stir.
3. Divide the mixture evenly between the cake papers. Bake for 18–20 minutes until risen and firm to touch. Allow to cool for a few minutes and then transfer to a wire rack. Allow to cool fully before icing.

TOPPING

1. Meanwhile, combine sugar, butter and orange juice in a bowl; beat with a whisk until light and fluffy. Combine with marmalade. Spoon glaze over each cupcake and top with a pecan piece.

3 eggs
½ cup butter, softened
1 cup superfine/caster sugar
¼ cup milk
1½ cups bakers/self-raising flour, sifted
½ teaspoon cocoa powder
zest of 1 small orange
juice of 1 small orange
¼ cup pecans, chopped

TOPPING

1½ cups confectioners'/icing sugar
½ cup butter, softened
¼ cup orange juice
2 tablespoons marmalade
12 pecan pieces

Ginger lime cupcakes

MAKES 12

3 eggs
½ cup butter, softened
1 cup superfine/caster sugar
½ cup buttermilk
2 cups bakers/self-raising flour,
    sifted
½ cup crystallised ginger, finely
    chopped
juice of ½ lime
zest of 1 lime

TOPPING
1¾ oz/50g crystallised ginger
½ cup confectioners'/icing sugar

1. Preheat the oven to 320°F/160°C. Line a 12-cupcake pan with cupcake papers. In a medium-sized bowl, lightly beat the eggs, add butter and sugar, then mix until light and fluffy.

2. Add buttermilk and flour, and stir to combine. Beat with an electric mixer for 2 minutes, until light and creamy. Add crystallised ginger, lime juice and zest, and mix thoroughly.

3. Divide the mixture evenly between the cake papers. Bake for 18–20 minutes until risen and firm to touch. Allow to cool for a few minutes and then transfer to a wire rack.

TOPPING
1. Top with slices of crystallised ginger and dust with sugar.

Double lemon cupcakes

MAKES 12

1. Preheat the oven to 350°F/180°C. Line a 12-cupcake pan with cupcake papers. In a medium-sized bowl, beat eggs, sugar, oil, lemon juice and zest with an electric mixer until thoroughly combined and creamy.

2. Sift the flour and baking powder into a bowl, then add the almond meal, candied lemon and egg mixture, and beat for 5 minutes.

3. Divide the mixture evenly between the cake cases. Bake for 20–25 minutes. Transfer to a wire rack. Allow to cool fully before icing.

TOPPING

1. Meanwhile, combine all ingredients except the food colouring and beat with an electric mixer for 5 minutes until creamy. Apply two-thirds of the topping to cupcakes. Add the yellow colouring to the remaining topping mixture and mix together. Top each cake with a smaller circle of yellow icing.

3 eggs
1¼ cups superfine/caster sugar
¾ cup vegetable oil
⅓ cup lemon juice
zest of 1 lemon
2¼ cups plain flour
2½ teaspoons baking powder
½ cup almond meal
½ cup candied lemon pieces,
  finely chopped

TOPPING
5 oz/150g confectioners'/icing
  sugar
zest 1 lemon
1 teaspoon lemon juice
3 oz/90g butter, softened
3 drops yellow food colouring

Lemon toffee cupcakes

MAKES 12

3 eggs
½ cup butter, softened
1 cup superfine/caster sugar
½ cup yoghurt
1 tablespoon lemon juice
zest of 1 lemon
2 cups bakers/self-raising flour,
    sifted
1 teaspoon vanilla extract
½ cup peanuts, crushed

TOPPING
½ cup superfine/caster sugar, for
    toffee
1½ cup confectioners'/icing
    sugar
½ cup butter, softened
6 pre-made meringue pieces,
    crushed

1. Preheat the oven to 320°F/160°C. Line a 12-cupcake pan with cupcake papers.
   In a medium-sized bowl, lightly beat the eggs, add butter and sugar, then mix until light and fluffy.

2. Add yoghurt, lemon juice, lemon zest, flour and vanilla, and stir to combine. Beat with an electric mixer for 2 minutes, until light and creamy. Fold in crushed peanuts.

3. Divide the mixture evenly between the cake papers. Bake for 18–20 minutes until risen and firm to touch. Allow to cool for a few minutes and then transfer to a wire rack. Allow to cool fully before icing.

TOPPING
1. Spread superfine sugar evenly on a greaseproof paper–lined baking tray, and bake at 400°F/200°C for approximately 25 minutes until toffee consistency forms. Cool until hardened.

2. Meanwhile, combine half the sugar and butter, mix with a wooden spoon, add remaining sugar and butter and beat with the spoon until light and fluffy. Spread onto cupcakes. Top with meringue and toffee pieces.

Orange choc swirl cupcakes

MAKES 12

1. Preheat the oven to 320°F/160°C. Line a 12-cupcake pan with cupcake papers. In a medium-sized bowl, lightly beat the eggs, add butter and sugar, then mix until light and fluffy.
2. Add milk and flour, and stir to combine. Beat with an electric mixer for 2 minutes, until light and creamy. Divide mixture into two bowls. Into bowl one, add orange juice and zest. Into bowl two, add cocoa powder. Put some of each mixture into each cake paper and gently stir with a skewer to get a marble effect.
3. Bake for 18–20 minutes until risen and firm to touch. Allow to cool for a few minutes and then transfer to a wire rack.

3 eggs
½ cup butter, softened
1 cup superfine/caster sugar
½ cup milk
2 cups bakers/self-raising flour, sifted
juice of ½ orange
zest of ½ orange
¼ cup cocoa powder

Lime and pistachio cupcakes

MAKES 12

3 eggs
½ cup butter, softened
1 cup superfine/caster sugar
½ cup milk
2 cups bakers/self-raising flour,
    sifted
1 teaspoon vanilla extract
½ cup pistachio nuts
juice of ½ lime
zest of 1 lime

TOPPING
1½ cups confectioners'/icing
    sugar
½ cup butter, softened
zest of 1 lime
½ cup pistachios

1. Preheat the oven to 320°F/160°C. Line a 12-cupcake pan with cupcake papers. In a medium-sized bowl, lightly beat the eggs, add butter and sugar, then mix until light and fluffy.
2. Add milk, flour and vanilla, and stir to combine. Beat with an electric mixer for 2 minutes, until light and creamy. Add pistachios, lime juice and zest, and combine.
3. Divide the mixture evenly between the cake papers. Bake for 18–20 minutes until risen and firm to touch. Allow to cool for a few minutes and then transfer to a wire rack. Allow to cool fully before icing.

TOPPING
1. Meanwhile, combine sugar and butter, mix with a wooden spoon and beat until light and fluffy. Add lime zest and pistachios and mix through. Spoon onto cupcakes in large, loose dollops.

Lemon sour cream
butter cupcakes

MAKES 12

1. Preheat the oven to 320°F/160°C. Line a 12-cupcake pan with cupcake papers. In a bowl, beat the butter, extract, essence, zest and sugar with an electric mixer until light and fluffy.
2. Beat in the eggs one at a time, scraping down the bowl between additions. Stir in half the flour and sour cream. Blend well. Mix in the remaining flour and sour cream, and mix thoroughly but gently.
3. Divide the mixture evenly between the cake papers. Bake for 18–20 minutes until risen and firm to touch. Allow to cool for a few minutes and then transfer to a wire rack. Allow to cool fully before icing.

TOPPING

1. Meanwhile, combine all ingredients and beat with an electric mixer for 5 minutes until creamy. Spoon mixture into a piping bag and decorate the top of each cake in a spiral.

4 oz/125g butter, softened
1 teaspoon vanilla extract
1 teaspoon lemon essence
zest 1 large lemon
1 cup superfine/caster sugar
3 eggs
1¼ cups plain flour
⅓ cup sour cream

TOPPING
5 oz/150g confectioners'/icing sugar
zest of 1 lemon
½ teaspoon lemon juice
4 oz/120g butter, softened

Jaffa choc cupcakes

MAKES 12

3 eggs
½ cup butter, softened
1 cup superfine/caster sugar
½ cup milk
1½ cups bakers/self-raising flour,
    sifted
1 teaspoon cocoa powder
1 teaspoon vanilla extract
juice 1 orange
zest 1 orange
¼ cup chocolate chips or flakes

TOPPING
2 cups confectioners'/icing sugar
1 cup butter, softened
⅓ cup orange juice
¼ cup chocolate powder or Milo

1. Preheat the oven to 320°F/160°C. Line a 12-cupcake pan with cupcake papers. In a medium-sized bowl, lightly beat the eggs, add butter and sugar, then mix until light and fluffy.

2. Add milk, flour, cocoa powder and vanilla, and stir to combine. Beat with an electric mixer for 2 minutes, until light and creamy.
Add juice, zest and chocolate chips.

3. Divide the mixture evenly between the cake papers. Bake for 18–20 minutes until risen and firm to touch. Allow to cool for a few minutes and then transfer to a wire rack. Allow to cool fully before icing.

TOPPING

1. Meanwhile, combine half of all the topping ingredients except the chocolate powder, mix with a wooden spoon, add remaining ingredients and beat with the spoon until light and fluffy. Add three-quarters of the chocolate powder and stir through. Top with the extra powder.

St Clement's cupcakes

MAKES 12

1. Preheat the oven to 350°F/180°C. Line a 12-cupcake pan with cupcake papers. Place all the ingredients except the zest in a bowl, and beat with an electric mixer on a medium speed for 5 minutes until pale and fluffy. Fold in the zest.
2. Divide the mixture evenly between the cake papers. Bake for 20–25 minutes until risen and firm to touch. Allow to cool for a few minutes and then transfer to a wire rack. Allow to cool fully before icing.

TOPPING

1. Meanwhile to make sugared citrus zest, coat the orange and lemon zest with superfine sugar and toss to thoroughly combine. Leave for at least 10 minutes.
2. Beat the butter with an electric mixer for 2 minutes and add milk, extracts and half of the confectioners' sugar. Beat for 3 minutes. Add the rest of the sugar and beat for a further 3 minutes.
3. Add mixture to piping bag, pipe onto cakes and top with the sugared citrus zest.

2 cups bakers/self-raising flour
2 cups superfine/caster sugar
9 oz/250g butter, softened
⅓ cup cornflour
4 eggs
1 cup buttermilk
1 teaspoon lemon extract
1 teaspoon orange extract
zest 1 orange
zest 1 lemon

TOPPING
zest 6 oranges
zest 6 lemons
1½ cups superfine/caster sugar
3½ oz/110g unsalted butter, softened
¼ cup milk
½ teaspoon orange extract
½ teaspoon lemon extract
4 cups confectioners'/icing sugar

Orange and ginger cupcakes

MAKES 12

5 eggs, separated
¾ cup superfine/caster sugar
3 teaspoons golden syrup
1 teaspoon orange extract
⅓ cup bakers/self-raising flour
⅓ cup cornflour
3 teaspoons ground ginger
½ teaspoon ground cinnamon
zest of 1½ oranges

TOPPING
6 oz/175g confectioners'/icing
  sugar
zest of ½ orange
1 teaspoon orange juice
4 oz/120g unsalted butter,
  softened
1 oz/30g crystallised ginger,
  sliced

1. Preheat the oven to 375°F/190°C. Line a 12-cupcake pan with cupcake papers. In a large bowl, whisk the egg whites with an electric mixer until soft peaks form. Gradually add the sugar and whisk until dissolved between additions. Add the egg yolks, syrup and extract.

2. Triple-sift the dry ingredients, add them to the egg mixture, add the zest and fold in gently.

3. Using an ice-cream scoop, divide mixture evenly between the cake papers. Bake for 10–15 minutes until risen and firm to touch. Allow to cool for a few minutes and then transfer to a wire rack. Allow to cool fully before icing.

TOPPING
1. Meanwhile, combine all ingredients except crystallised ginger and beat with an electric mixer on high for 5 minutes until creamy. Apply the topping to cupcakes and place a cluster of the ginger pieces on top of each cake.

novelty cupcakes

Here's a chapter to put a sparkle in a child's eye and a smile on your face. No cupcake book would be complete without a set of playful recipes reminding you of all the celebrations that cupcakes can help you with. Keep a supply of sugared decorations in a few of life's more standard themes on hand— baby showers, national celebration day, Christmas and, of course, birthday candles.

Violet Baby Cupcakes

Butterfly Cupcakes

Easter Choc Cupcakes

Playtime Cupcakes

Choc Chic Cupcakes

Parsnip Passion Cupcakes

Chrissy Top Cupcakes

Vanilla Rudolph Cupcakes

Chai Chai Cupcakes

Violet baby cupcakes

3 eggs
½ cup butter, softened
1 cup superfine/caster sugar
½ cup milk
1½ cups bakers/self-raising flour,
  sifted
1 teaspoon vanilla extract

TOPPING
1½ cups confectioners'/icing
  sugar
½ cup butter, softened
1 tablespoon water
6 drops purple food colouring
3 teaspoons coloured sugar
  sprinkles
12 miniature baby rattle toys
  (available from cake decoration
  stores)

1. Preheat the oven to 320°F/160°C. Line a 12-cupcake pan with cupcake papers. In a medium-sized bowl, lightly beat the eggs, add butter and sugar, then mix until light and fluffy.

2. Add milk, flour and vanilla, and stir to combine. Beat with an electric mixer for 2 minutes, until light and creamy.

3. Divide the mixture evenly between the cake papers. Bake for 18–20 minutes until risen and firm to touch. Allow to cool for a few minutes and then transfer to a wire rack. Allow to cool fully before icing.

TOPPING
1. Meanwhile, thoroughly combine the topping ingredients. Using the back of a teaspoon, apply the topping to cupcakes. Top with purple sugar sprinkles and a novelty toy.

Butterfly cupcakes

MAKES 12

1. Preheat the oven to 320°F/160°C. Line a 12-cupcake pan with cupcake papers. In a medium-sized bowl, lightly beat the eggs, add butter and sugar, then mix until light and fluffy.
2. Add milk, flour and vanilla, and stir to combine. Beat with an electric mixer for 2 minutes, until light and creamy.
3. Divide the mixture evenly between the cake papers. Bake for 18–20 minutes until risen and firm to touch. Allow to cool for a few minutes and then transfer to a wire rack. Allow to cool fully before icing.

TOPPING

1. Meanwhile, combine all topping ingredients, mix with a wooden spoon until well combined, then beat with the spoon until light and fluffy.
2. Place mixture into a piping bag, and set aside. Using a sharp knife, cut a 10cm circle into the centre of each cupcake, slicing the top off. Cut these circles in half and set aside. Fill the centre of each cupcake with icing, and stand the two half-circles of cake upright, to form wings.

3 eggs
½ cup butter, softened
1 cup superfine/caster sugar
½ cup milk
1½ cups bakers/self-raising flour, sifted
1 teaspoon vanilla extract

TOPPING
1½ cups confectioners'/icing sugar
1 teaspoon vanilla extract
½ cup butter, softened

Easter choc cupcakes

MAKES 12

3 eggs
½ cup butter, softened
1 cup superfine/caster sugar
½ cup milk
1½ cups bakers/self-raising flour,
    sifted
1 teaspoon vanilla extract
7 oz/200g dark chocolate pieces
1 tablespoon cocoa powder

TOPPING
3½ oz/100g dark chocolate
1 tablespoon butter, softened
⅓ cup cream, thickened
½ cup butter, softened
1½ cup confectioners'/icing
    sugar
36 small easter eggs

1. Preheat the oven to 320°F/160°C. Line a 12-cupcake pan with cupcake papers. In a medium-sized bowl, lightly beat the eggs, add butter and sugar, then mix until light and fluffy.
2. Add milk, flour aand vanilla, and stir to combine. Add remaining ingredients. Beat with an electric mixer for 2 minutes, until light and creamy.
3. Divide the mixture evenly between the cake papers. Bake for 18–20 minutes until risen and firm to touch. Allow to cool for a few minutes and then transfer to a wire rack. Allow to cool fully before icing.

TOPPING
1. Meanwhile, combine the chocolate and tablespoon of butter in a medium-sized saucepan over medium heat. As the mixture begins to melt, add cream slowly, then reduce heat to low, stirring constantly until mixture thickens. Remove from heat and cool.
2. Combine butter and sugar, mix with a wooden spoon, then beat with the spoon until light and fluffy. Add melted chocolate and combine. Spoon onto cupcakes and place 3 easter eggs on top of each cupcake.

Playtime cupcakes

MAKES 12

1. Preheat the oven to 320°F/160°C. Line a 12-cupcake pan with cupcake papers. In a medium-sized bowl, lightly beat the eggs, add butter and sugar, then mix until light and fluffy.
2. Add milk, flour and vanilla, and stir to combine. Beat with an electric mixer for 2 minutes, until light and creamy.
3. Divide the mixture evenly between the cake papers. Bake for 18–20 minutes until risen and firm to touch. Allow to cool for a few minutes and then transfer to a wire rack. Allow to cool fully before icing.

TOPPING

1. Meanwhile, using a rolling pin roll out the fondant to 1/8in/3mm thick. Using a biscuit cutter or small sharp knife, cut small circles and use to top cupcakes. Draw numbers on top with the gel icing.

3 eggs
½ cup butter, softened
1 cup superfine/caster sugar
½ cup milk
1½ cups bakers/self-raising flour, sifted
1 teaspoon vanilla extract

TOPPING
7 oz/200g coloured fondant
gel icing

Choc chic cupcakes

MAKES 12

3 eggs
½ cup butter, softened
1 cup superfine/caster sugar
½ cup milk
1½ cups bakers/self-raising flour,
    sifted
1 teaspoon vanilla extract
7 oz/200g dark chocolate pieces
1 tablespoon cocoa powder

TOPPING
3½ oz/100g dark chocolate
1 tablespoon butter, softened
⅓ cup cream, thickened
1 cup butter, softened
1 cup confectioners'/icing sugar
novelty chickens (available from
    cake decoration shops)

1. Preheat the oven to 320°F/160°C. Line a 12-cupcake pan with cupcake papers. In a medium-sized bowl, lightly beat the eggs, add butter and sugar, then mix until light and fluffy.
2. Add milk, flour and vanilla, and stir to combine. Add remaining ingredients. Beat with an electric mixer for 2 minutes, until light and creamy.
3. Divide the mixture evenly between the cake papers. Bake for 18–20 minutes until risen and firm to touch. Allow to cool for a few minutes and then transfer to a wire rack. Allow to cool fully before icing.

TOPPING
1. Meanwhile, combine the chocolate and tablespoon of butter in a medium-sized saucepan over medium heat. As the mixture begins to melt, add cream slowly, and reduce heat to low, stirring constantly until mixture thickens Remove from heat and cool.
2. Combine butter and sugar, mix with a wooden spoon, then beat with the spoon until light and fluffy. Add melted chocolate, combine, and spoon onto cupcakes. Add novelty chickens to the top of each cupcake.

Parsnip passion cupcakes

MAKES 24

1. Preheat the oven to 350°F/180°C. Line two 12-cupcake pans with cupcake papers. Using a wooden spoon, mix the flour, sugars, baking powder, bicarbonate of soda, cinnamon and salt. Add the oil and eggs and beat until thoroughly combined. Mix in the parsnips and pineapple and beat well.
2. Divide the mixture evenly between the cake papers. Bake for 18–20 minutes until risen and firm to touch. Allow to cool for a few minutes and then transfer to a wire rack. Allow to cool fully before icing.

8 oz/225g bakers/self-raising flour
2½ oz/75g superfine/caster sugar
2½ oz/75g soft brown sugar
1 teaspoon baking powder
1 teaspoon baking soda
1 teaspoon ground cinnamon
1 teaspoon salt
5 fl oz/150ml sunflower oil
2 eggs, beaten
4 oz/125g parsnips, grated
7 oz/200g canned crushed pineapple, drained

TOPPING

1. Meanwhile, mix the sugar, mascarpone, lemon juice and vanilla extract with a fork until smooth. Spread over the cakes.
2. Cut out mini parsnip shapes from the yellow fondant icing. Pare strips of green fondant with a vegetable peeler, then twist round a clean pencil to curl. Gently slip the curls off the pencil and set aside to dry. Arrange the parsnips on top of the cakes.

TOPPING

9½ oz/275g confectioners'/icing sugar, sifted
4 oz/125g mascarpone
4 teaspoons lemon juice
2 drops vanilla extract
1 box coloured fondant icing

Chrissy top cupcakes

MAKES 12

3 eggs
½ cup unsalted butter, softened
½ cup superfine/caster sugar
⅓ cup unsweetened pineapple
    juice
1 cup all-purpose/plain flour,
    sifted
1½ cups candied fruit, finely
    chopped
⅔ cup raisins, chopped
¼ cup pitted dates, finely
    chopped
¾ teaspoon baking powder
½ teaspoon salt
½ teaspoon vanilla extract

TOPPING

1½ cups confectioners'/icing
    sugar
1 teaspoon lemon extract
½ cup butter, softened
1 tablespoon brandy
candied novelty holly (available
    from specialist cake decoration
    stores)

1. Preheat the oven to 320°F/160°C. Line a 12-cupcake pan with cupcake papers. In a medium-sized bowl, lightly beat the eggs, add butter and sugar, then mix until light and fluffy.

2. Add pineapple juice and flour, and stir to combine. Add remaining ingredients. Beat with an electric mixer for 2 minutes, until light and creamy.

3. Divide the mixture evenly between the cake papers. Bake for 18–20 minutes until risen and firm to touch. Allow to cool for a few minutes and then transfer to a wire rack. Allow to cool fully before icing.

TOPPING

1. Meanwhile, combine half-quantities of all the topping ingredients except for the novelty holly, and mix with a wooden spoon. Add remaining ingredients and beat with the spoon until light and fluffy.

2. Put icing into a piping bag with a medium-sized plain nozzle and pipe onto fruit cakes. Top with candied novelty holly.

Vanilla rudolph cupcakes

MAKES 12

1. Preheat the oven to 320°F/160°C. Line a 12-cupcake pan with cupcake papers. In a medium-sized bowl, lightly beat the eggs, add butter and sugar, then mix until light and fluffy.
2. Add milk, flour and vanilla, and stir to combine. Beat with an electric mixer for 2 minutes, until light and creamy.
3. Divide the mixture evenly between the cake papers. Bake for 18–20 minutes until risen and firm to touch. Allow to cool for a few minutes and then transfer to a wire rack. Allow to cool fully before icing.

TOPPING

1. Meanwhile, combine the chocolate and butter in a medium-sized saucepan over medium heat. As the mixture begins to melt, reduce heat to low, and add cream slowly, stirring constantly until the mixture thickens. Remove from heat and cool. Decorate the top of each cake with topping and a novelty reindeer.

3 eggs
½ cup butter, softened
1 cup superfine/caster sugar
½ cup milk
1½ cups bakers/self-raising flour, sifted
2 teaspoons vanilla extract

TOPPING
3½ oz/100g dark chocolate
1 tablespoon butter, softened
⅓ cup thickened cream
novelty reindeers (available from specialist cake decoration stores)

Chai chai cupcakes

MAKES 12

¼ cup hot water
¼ cup chai mixture (Indian spiced
  tea)
3 eggs
½ cup butter, softened
1 cup superfine/caster sugar
¼ cup milk
1½ cups bakers/self-raising flour,
  sifted
1 teaspoon vanilla extract
1 teaspoon cinnamon
1 teaspoon nutmeg

TOPPING
¼ cup raw sugar
2 tablespoons warm water
cinnamon sugar
12 star anises

1. Preheat the oven to 320°F/160°C. Line a 12-cupcake pan with cupcake papers. In a small bowl, add hot water to the spiced tea mixture, stand for 15 minutes, strain and set aside. In a medium-sized bowl, lightly beat the eggs, add butter and sugar, then mix until light and fluffy.

2. Add milk and flour, and stir to combine. Add remaining ingredients. Beat with an electric mixer for 2 minutes, until light and creamy. Add chai tea and stir through.

3. Divide the mixture evenly between the cake papers. Bake for 18–20 minutes until risen and firm to touch. Allow to cool for a few minutes and then transfer to a wire rack. Allow to cool fully before icing.

TOPPING

1. Meanwhile, combine the raw sugar and water in a small bowl, mix with a wooden spoon, spoon onto cupcakes and sprinkle with cinnamon sugar. Decorate each cupcake with a single star anise.

muffins

Muffins are a great, no-fuss way to turn a few pantry ingredients into quick snacks. These little treats travel easily and with the addition of fruits and nuts, are nutritious as well. A freshly baked fruit and nut muffin makes a great breakfast on the go. It takes very little effort to get a batch into the oven while you brew the morning coffee or take a shower.
The chocolate muffin in any form is a crowd-pleaser, a favourite for the kids and adults alike. In general, it's easy to turn chocolate into a delicious baked treat!

Mixed fruit muffins

MAKES 12

2½ cups bakers/self-raising flour
1 teaspoon ground cinnamon
1 cup rolled oats
⅔ cup brown sugar
13 fl oz/375ml milk
2 eggs, lightly beaten
1 teaspoon vanilla extract
2 tablespoons vegetable oil
3½ oz/100g thick vanilla yoghurt
9 oz/250g mixed fresh fruit, cut
*   into small pieces*

1. Preheat the oven to 400°F/200°C.
    Grease a 12-muffin pan. Sift the flour
    and cinnamon into a large bowl, then
    stir in the rolled oats and brown sugar.
    Make a well in the centre of the
    mixture.
2. Put the milk, eggs, vanilla extract, oil
    and yoghurt in a jug and whisk to
    combine.
3. Pour the liquid ingredients and half of
    the mixed fresh fruit into the well and
    mix until just combined – do not
    over-mix.
4. Three-quarter-fill the muffin cups with
    mixture, and scatter the remaining fruit
    mixture over the muffins. Bake for
    25–30 minutes or until the muffins are
    risen and have started to come away
    from the side of the pan.

Chocafé muffins

MAKES 12

1. Preheat the oven to 375°F/190°C. Grease a 12-muffin pan. Beat eggs, sugar and vanilla extract together until thick and creamy. The mixture should hold a figure-of-eight shape when it reaches this stage.
2. Melt the butter. Sift flour, baking powder, cocoa powder and coffee into the egg mixture and fold in with butter.
3. Three-quarter-fill muffin cups with mixture. Bake for 12–15 minutes or until muffins spring back when lightly touched. Allow to cool for 5 minutes before turning onto a wire rack.

TOPPING
1. Cut a ¼in/1cm slit in the top of each muffin.
2. Cut the chocolate mints in half diagonally and push the cut side into the slit in each muffin. Dust with sugar and sprinkle with grated chocolate.

4 eggs
¾ cup superfine/caster sugar
1 teaspoon vanilla extract
1¾ oz/50g butter, softened
½ cup all-purpose/plain flour
1 teaspoon baking powder
½ cup cocoa powder
2 tablespoons instant coffee

TOPPING
6 x 1½ in/4cm chocolate mint squares
confectioners'/icing sugar, for dusting
chocolate, finely grated

Index

First published in 2012 by
New Holland Publishers
London • Sydney • Cape Town • Auckland
www.newhollandpublishers.com

Garfield House 86–88 Edgware Road London W2 2EA United Kingdom
1/66 Gibbes Street Chatswood NSW 2067 Australia
Wembley Square First Floor Solan Road Gardens Cape Town 8001 South Africa
218 Lake Road Northcote Auckland New Zealand

A catalogue record of this book is available at the British Library and the National Library of Australia.

ISBN: 9781742573618

Managing Director: Fiona Schultz
Publishing Director: Lliane Clarke
Design: Stephanie Foti
Production Director: Olga Dementiev
Printer: Toppan Leefung Printing Limited

10 9 8 7 6 5 4 3 2

Follow New Holland Publishers on
Facebook: www.facebook.com/NewHollandPublishers

UK £9.99
US $14.99